Adventures in a TV Nation

MICHAEL MOORE & KATHLEEN GLYNN

PAN BOOKS

Grateful acknowledgement is made to David Litwinsky for permission to reprint the letter written to him by the U.S. Postal Service.

Photo & Illustration Credits
All photos courtesy of Columbia TriStar Television, except the following:
p.3; Danny Field; p. 4: NBC; p. 7: Gerry Goodstein; p. 10: NBC; p. 11: BBC; p. 12: Gerry Goodstein; p. 13: Gerry Goodstein; p. 40: Kathleen Glynn; pp. 41, 42, 44, 45: Joe Rosen for NBC; p. 48: (top) Jay Martel, (bottom left) Robert Flanagan (bottom right) Todd Rutt; p. 59: Todd Rutt; p. 64: Courtesy Philip Morris; p. 65: Courtesy Colgate-Palmolive; p. 68: Courtesy Alex Trotman; p. 115: © 1992 Tracy Cox; p.130: David Royle; p. 155: (left) NBC/Paul Drinkwater, (right) NBC; pp. 184, 185: Joanne Doroshow; p. 190: NBC; p. 201: Craig T. Mathew, Mathew Photographic Services; p. 203: Damon J. Hartley; p. 213: Kathleen Glynn; p. 221: Joseph Reyes, Mayor's Photo Office

First published in the United States in 1998 by HarperCollins Publishers, New York

First published in Great Britain in 1998 by Boxtree

This edition published 2002 by Pan Books
an imprint of Pan Macmillan Ltd
Pan Macmillan, 20 New Wharf Road
London N1 9RR
Basingstoke and Oxford
Associated companies throughout the world

ISBN 0 330 41914 5

9 8 7 6 5 4

A CIP catalogue record for this book is available from the British Library.

Printed and bound by Mackays of Chatham Plc, Chatham, Kent

Adventures in a TV Nation

for Natalie Rose

Contents

Introduction

This is a book about how a group of people went after corporate crooks with a seven-foot crime-fighting chicken, hired a former KGB agent to make sure Nixon was *really* dead, and got the warring factions in Bosnia to put down their guns, slice up a pizza, and sing the Barney song to each other.

And it all ended up on primetime television, on networks owned by General Electric (NBC) and Rupert Murdoch (Fox).

The show was called *TV Nation*. It was hailed by the critics as "brilliant," "subversive," and "the best show on TV in the past 30 years." It had ten million weekly viewers and beat its competition on the other three networks in the twenty-five- to fifty-four-year-old audience every week it was on the air. It was nominated twice for a primetime Emmy Award and won the Emmy for Outstanding Informational Series for the 1994 season.

After seventeen episodes, it was gone.

When *TV Nation* went off the air, the Fox network received fifty-five thousand letters from viewers demanding its renewal. No TV show on that network had ever received so much unsolicited mail. Demonstrations were held in front of local Fox stations by supporters of the show in over thirty cities. Forty thousand people joined a *TV Nation* fan club on the Internet.

Think of this book as a consumer's guide to raising hell and having fun while doing it. Who said citizen participation and political action has to be limited to the politicians and the fat cats who subsidize them? Haven't you been wanting to take on the system that has made your life more and more miserable—or at least later and later for dinner every night? Wouldn't you like, for once, to see the boss of your company, the mayor of your town, or that worthless HMO of yours get their comeuppance?

If so, this is your book.

You need not ever have seen *TV Nation* to enjoy what you're about to read. Hell, we didn't even see half the shows ourselves considering the way the networks kept moving them around the schedule, or preempted them for summer preseason football games.

Throughout this book you will read the word "we." That "we" represents the *TV Nation* staff, a dedicated, energetic, wickedly funny, and intelligent group that ceaselessly turned in top-notch work. They are listed on page 239. The authors of this chronicle, Kathleen Glynn and Michael Moore, created and produced *TV Nation*. Mike is the one who watches too much TV, and Kathleen is the one who would rather be reading. A perfect combination, *we* thought, for a book based on a TV show based on real life.

So, enjoy reading this book, and if inspiration strikes, put it down, leave the house, and get involved. Right now, in your own town, you could be having your own *TV Nation* adventure.

Adventures in a TV Nation

Who Let
This Show
on the Air?

It is true that the best things that happen to you happen when you least expect them. Or, in our case, when we actively try to avoid them.

In 1989, a low-budget documentary we made, *Roger & Me*, a film about what General Motors did to our hometown of Flint, Michigan, became a huge success. It was a complete surprise. The film was shot over a three-year period in whatever spare time we had with what little money we had. Our intent was to finish it, hop in a van, and drive around the country showing it in union halls, community centers, and church groups. We silk-screened some T-shirts and took them to sell at our first film festival so we could afford the trip back home. Instead, our film was bought by Warner Bros., and eventually shown in nearly two thousand theaters.

After *Roger & Me,* the head of Warner Bros. television asked to meet with us about ideas for creating a television series. We thought, "TV? Who wants to do TV?" We wanted to make movies! The meeting never took place.

Our next feature-length film was a long time coming. Michael had written *Canadian Bacon* in the summer of 1991, but Warner Bros. passed on it. So did every other studio. The screenplay for *Canadian Bacon* was a farcical takeoff on the Gulf War. It was deemed "too political" by most of the executives who read it. Michael made numerous trips to L.A. to pitch the movie in one unsuccessful meeting after another.

It was on one of those visits to Hollywood, in November of 1992, when one morning Michael found himself in his hotel room raiding the minibar and watching *The Price Is Right.* The phone rang with a call from a network executive at NBC.

"We just wanted to say we really liked *Roger & Me* and we were wondering if you had any ideas for a television show."

"Uh, sure!" Michael replied, not having a single TV idea in his head.

"Great! We'd like to set up a meeting with you and our president of entertainment, Warren Littlefield. How does this afternoon look?"

"Uh, let me check." Mike fumbled around, trying to find the remote control to turn down the volume on the television set. "Yeah, this afternoon looks open."

"Good, we'll see you at four."

Panic set in. We had no ideas for a TV show and even if we did, we didn't want to do one. We wanted to make *Canadian Bacon.*

On the half-hour drive to Burbank that afternoon, Michael cranked up the heavy metal and we talked on the car phone trying to think up something for the meeting. It was then, with the car radio blasting out Metallica, that we came up with the idea of *TV Nation.* It would be a humorous magazine show but with one distinct difference—it would have a point of view. It would stand for something, instead of pretending to play it down the middle of the road, as most other newsmagazine shows do. It would side with working people against corporations.

Who would advertise on such a show? No one, we thought! We figured that the meeting should be over in a matter of minutes. Mike seemed relieved knowing that *no* network, let alone NBC, would ever pick up *TV Nation*.

Upon arriving at NBC, Mike was told that the meeting was in the commissary. A good sign, Mike thought. Very low-key. He was greeted by his agent as well as an executive from TriStar Television, Eric Tannenbaum. Eric offered to join Mike upstairs and present TriStar as the studio for the potential TV show. After all the formalities, Eric asked, "By the way, what *is* your idea for a TV show?" Mike pitched the idea for *TV Nation*.

"I thought you were going to come up with a blue-collar *Northern Exposure*," Mike's agent lamented. "They are not going to like this idea."

"I like it," Tannenbaum countered. "It's funny and it's different."

Eric Tannenbaum, president,
Columbia TriStar Television.

Warren Littlefield, president, NBC Entertainment.

Mike was concerned that Tannenbaum approved of the concept. But he reassured himself with, "What does Tannenbaum know? He doesn't run a network! He's just a nice guy with a good sense of humor from a studio. Not to worry."

The three of them went upstairs to see the NBC president. In the room with Warren Littlefield were various vice-presidents of development and programming. After polite introductions they sat down and Mike began to describe the show.

"It would be a cross between *60 Minutes* and Fidel Castro on laughing gas."

The suits sat up in their chairs, interested.

"The show would be the most liberal thing ever seen on TV. In fact, it would go beyond 'liberals' because liberals are a bunch of wimps and haven't gotten us anything. This show would go boldly where no one has gone before."

All smiles in the room. "Tell us more!"

"The correspondents would look like shit. I mean, they'd look as if they were either on their way to Betty Ford or had just spent a year working at Taco Bell—or both."

"In other words," one of the junior executives chimed in, "a *real* show, by *real* people, for *real* people."

Excited executive smiles all around again. What was happening here? Didn't they realize that we didn't want to be on television, that these ideas would all spell suicide for the network?

Obviously not.

Mike had no choice but to go for the kill.

"Each week we'll pick one of our advertisers and go after them like a barracuda. They won't know what hit them. Then we'll go after organized religion, starting with our fellow Catholics. I've got one idea where I'll go to confession in twenty different churches and confess the same exact sin to see who gives out the harshest penances. We'll run the results and call it 'A Consumers Guide to the Confessional.'"

There was a pause of silence in the room—and then everyone burst out laughing. "That's the funniest idea I've ever heard," Littlefield exclaimed through his belly laugh. "Genius!"

"No," Mike pleaded, "think of all the hate mail you'll get from your Catholic viewers—including me! As a former altar boy and seminarian, I'd hate you to run this offensive piece!"

"Mike," Littlefield said, "Catholics are the ones with the sense of humor. You know that. They'll love this!"

Everyone around the room nodded in agreement. Thank-yous were exchanged, Tannenbaum patted Mike on the back for "hitting a home run," and Mike drove back to his West Hollywood hotel, wondering what had gone wrong. By the time he made it to his room, NBC had already called and left a message. It read: "*Pilot has green light. Budget around one mil. Call agent.*"

We were stunned. Two years of trying to get a movie made with no luck, and in less than fifteen minutes in Burbank, we get a million bucks to produce a prime-time TV show. This is a very strange business, indeed.

In January, 1994, we began making the *TV Nation* pilot for NBC. We didn't have any experience or a clue as to what we were doing. We

TV NATION...
   Disgruntled but Unaimed
TV NATION...
   Getting Even
   It Beats a Real Job
   Stop Us Before We Kill Again
   We Eat What We Kill
   Slippery When Wet
   We've Passed the Urine Test
   Just Say Know
   Start the Insanity
   Point That Thing Somewhere Else
   Why the Canabalism?
   Ugly When Naked

TV NATION What's It To You? . CATCH PHRAS
TV Nation
   What Do We Know
TV Nation
   You Know   TV NATION
TV Nation   THE TRUTH?
   It Couldn't Hurt
TV Nation
   Dammit!
TV Nation
   It'll Just Hurt a Little
TV Nation
   So What
TV Nation
   Turn & Cough

Mike's scribbled notes for TV Nation slogans on a dinner napkin.

called up some friends: Joanne Doroshow (coproducer of a documentary on the U.S. invasion of Panama that won an Academy Award), Pam Yates (Pam had also won an Academy Award), Paco de Onís, Jim Czarnecki (a funny guy who had worked on a Saturday morning TV show, *Pee-wee's Playhouse*. That made him the most qualified of the bunch), and David Royle, a documentary producer who had just finished a series on the Mafia. They would all be our segment producers. We hired Jerry Kupfer to be our supervising producer. He had some experience on *Showtime at the Apollo,* and he had set up some public radio stations on Indian reservations.

To find the show's correspondents, we conducted the normal casting sessions one does for a new show. Except this show wasn't "normal." There had never been anything like *TV Nation* on the air before. Was it news? Was it entertainment? Even NBC didn't know and ended up putting us in their "drama" division.

TV Nation was to be a combination of documentary and humor; the journalists we interviewed weren't very funny, and the comedians we auditioned for the most part knew little about what

was going on in the world. This part of putting the show together was very difficult.

In the end, we convinced Merrill Markoe, one of the key creators of the Letterman show, filmmaker Rusty Cundieff, who had just made a hilarious satire called *Fear of a Black Hat,* and actress/comedian Janeane Garofalo to be our on-air "reporters."

We decided that each hour program (forty-five actual minutes without the commercials) would have five eight-minute stories, plus introductions by Mike. The criteria we set were that each seg-

The crew sets up for the Confession shoot.

ment had to show the viewer something he or she had never seen before on TV; aggressively take on the powers that be, whoever they may be; and give us some sort of comic relief as we considered the horror of what we were actually watching.

It didn't take long to come up with the six segments we would shoot (hoping that five of them would turn out to be OK). The stories revolved around these ideas:

1. Is it easier for a convicted white murderer or an award-winning black actor to get a taxi in New York City?
2. Let's fire everyone on the show and move it to Mexico to take advantage of the North American Free Trade Agreement (NAFTA).
3. Let's buy a home in newly reopened Love Canal.
4. Appleton, Minnesota: They built a prison to revitalize their economy, but can't find any prisoners.
5. Mike travels to the former USSR to find the missile they had pointed at his hometown during the Cold War.
6. And, Mike's idea about going to confession.

We decided to go with the first five stories. Mike had second thoughts about violating the sacrament of confession, so he asked Janeane to do the piece. As a recovering Catholic, she was more than willing. But when the segment was finished, Mike was confident he would burn in eternal hell if this segment ever ran, so he spiked it.

Two other short pieces were killed by the network. One was called "The Corporate Minute." The idea was that each week we would make a one-minute satirical commercial "saluting" a business. Our first choice was Dow Chemical. With patriotic music in the background, we lauded the company that has been sued for polluting the environment, causing health problems for women, and general death and destruction in Vietnam. NBC and TriStar decided that some viewers might actually think it was a real commercial sponsored by Dow.

The other piece was called "Lie of the Week." We were going to use a voice-activated lie detector, attach it to a TV, and then run a test on what the news tells us each night. Either the machine didn't work that well or the network news division had some explainin' to do because when we tested this, the machine registered a lie in nearly every report on the news. Needless to say, the plug was pulled on this segment.

In between each segment, we decided that we would conduct an actual poll of the American public—but not with the same dull and unrevealing questions that are asked in your typical Gallup poll (see Appendix A). We hired a man named Robin Widgery from Flint who had his own polling firm and we had him call a sample of 204 people from around the country and ask them questions that would yield results like "67 percent of Perot voters believe that *Forrest Gump* was a documentary" or "51 percent of all Republicans believe that if dolphins were really smart, they'd find a way out of those nets."

65% of all Americans believe that frozen pizza will never be any good and there's nothing science can do about it.

Source: Widgery & Associates. Margin of error within 9%. From a telephone survey of 204 Americans, Spring 1993.

We also decided that, instead of having a studio audience or a fake set, we would shoot the introduction of all segments, including the opening and closing of the show, with Mike hanging out in Times Square.

Finally, we wanted a cool title sequence that would open each show. We hired graphic designer Chris Harvey to come up with the images and the music group tomandandy to write the *TV Nation* theme. We told them it should be a cross between Metallica and the *Leave It to Beaver* theme song.

We completed the pilot in three months, then brought it out to NBC in Los Angeles. On the day it was screened, all the executives of the network sat in the room and laughed nonstop at all five segments. As the lights went up, one suit asked another, "Can we sell any advertising on this thing?" They decided to screen the show for a focus group. These instant critics gave *TV Nation* the highest marks. NBC then decided to test it with the entire town of Scranton, Pennsylvania. It scored the highest of all pilots that season. Unfortunately, there was no room in the fall schedule for our show. The prospects of an audience ever seeing *TV Nation* were bleak.

So, Mike went back to trying to get *Canadian Bacon* made, but with a new tool to convince Hollywood—the tape of the *TV Nation* pilot. We loaned the pilot to John Candy and Alan Alda, and they loved it. We then showed them the script of *Canadian Bacon* and they agreed to star in it. With their names attached to the project, we were immediately able to raise the funds to make the movie, which we did in the fall and early winter of 1993.

Then an odd, lucky thing happened. You don't usually think of the person who runs the BBC in Great Britain as being an avid devourer of *TV Guide*. But Michael Jackson (no relation to The Gloved One), then head of BBC–2, was reading *TV Guide* one day and noticed a one-sentence gossip item which said that Michael Moore had made a pilot for NBC. Jackson, who had seen *Roger & Me*, was intrigued. Wondering what this pilot could be about, he called NBC and asked them to send him a tape. After viewing it, he called TriStar and NBC and told them the BBC would like to buy the show.

You could see the lightbulbs going off in the network craniums in L.A. "You know, if the British like it, it must be good!"

On the night after Christmas 1993, we received a phone call from Eric Tannenbaum of TriStar Television.

"What do you think about doing a summer season of *TV Nation* on NBC?" he asked. "They want to do it and the BBC wants to do it. They'll share the cost."

Michael Jackson, the man
who finally made it happen.

We were stunned. We thought the show would never see the light of day. We immediately accepted the offer.

A month later, we were setting up our production office in New York. Virtually everyone who had worked on the pilot came back to be a part of the show. On the first day of work, we gathered everyone together and gave them, essentially, the following pep talk:

"All of us need to behave as if we'll never work in television again. Because, if we do this show right, nobody will ever want us. It will be too dangerous to have us around. 'Oh, you worked on that show that pissed off all the sponsors!' That's what they'll say. So, if you want to work on *20/20* or *Live with Regis and Kathie Lee* after this show is over, we suggest you leave now and apply there. Because they will not want you after this show airs. This is not a place to build a résumé. We are here to produce a show that will be brutally honest and devastatingly funny. We will not make any friends in Congress or Corporate America. We will not lie to the viewer. This is a rare chance for all of us who usually do not have a voice in the media to have our voices heard. For one hour each week, we're going to give the average person like ourselves the

Mike works with cameraman Jean de Segonzac on the Confession shoot.

chance to watch a show that is clearly on THEIR side. They'll know it and love us for it—but we'll never work in television again."

Just a little pick-me-up to get things going right on the first day!

The results that followed are chronicled in this book. Thanks to the hard work and take-no-prisoners attitude of the staff, we were able to make a bit of television history.

And all of this because we never really wanted to do a TV show. Go figure.

2

Love Night

America is a country filled with hate groups, organizations that are out to harm, remove, maim, and kill those people who have a skin tone that is not white or a religious belief that is not Protestant. According to research conducted by the Anti-Defamation League, these crazies can be found in nearly every state in the union.

Consequently, there are also many people opposed to these hate groups. They do good work. Through protest, monitoring, and legislation, they labor to limit the activities of these bigoted organizations. Yet, in spite of such efforts, the hate groups have grown by leaps and bounds. There are now fifty different militia groups in our home state of Michigan alone.

Their success comes from preying on those who have been hit hardest by the economy and need someone to blame for their hard times. Instead of blaming Corporate America and the inequitable economic system we have, many people unfortunately fall for the propaganda of the right wing. From Newt Gingrich to the nutty white-separatist groups, they have easy answers for those who have seen their American Dream go up in smoke: Blame the welfare mothers! Blame the illegal immigrants! Hate! Fear! Justice for all TRUE Americans!!

At *TV Nation*, we decided that one good way to counteract this idiocy was to simply ridicule these groups. We hoped that viewers watching our take on these people would think they were complete lunatics and would never want to be part of their movement.

What these groups needed was not more hate, but love. Yes, love. Love is all they need.

We chose four different hate groups and, throughout one show, sent our emissaries of love to visit them. Our targets were a Klan rally in Georgia, an Aryan Nations convention in Idaho, the offices of the antiabortion group Operation Rescue, and Senator Jesse Helms. (Helms is not a group, but an entire hate movement unto himself.)

With Minnie Ripperton's "Lovin' You" playing in the background, here's how it all unfolded.

Love Night for the Ku Klux Klan

On a hot July day, the Grand Knights of the Georgia Ku Klux Klan were holding a rally on the steps of the courthouse in Cumming, Georgia. Parents dressed their kids in sheets and hoods, grandparents in Klan garb held babies while speakers praised God "for AIDS and its continued elimination of all faggots." They shouted "gook!" and "nigger!" and "kike!" while the crowd cheered and the American flag blew in the breeze.

Suddenly, the rally was interrupted by the *TV Nation* "Love Night Mariachi Band." A group of Mexican American men with guitars and horns strode toward the stage playing and singing "Amor." They were greeted with catcalls, boos, and racial epithets. One man attending the rally confronted them and demanded that they prove their "American citizenship."

Then, the *TV Nation* "Love Night Cheerleaders," a group of African American women from Spelman College, began their love cheers to the Klan.

"Two, four, six, eight!
Try to love instead of hate!"

"Hey! Hey! Hey!
K! K! K!
Put aside your hate today!"

"Look to the left!
Look to the right!
Love all people
Black *and* white!"

The TV Nation Love Night Cheerleaders.

"Be really cool! Be really neat!
Put away that tired old sheet!"

"One, two, three, four, we just want to love you more!
Five, six, seven, eight, even if you're filled with hate!"

To finally send them over the edge, we set up a kissing booth, offering the hooded hunks a free smooch in the hopes that a little pucker might get them to see the error of their ways.

Needless to say, the white supremacists did not take too kindly to all this love. In fact, it made them hate more. They screamed "nigger!" at the cheerleaders, started to push around the mariachi singers, and just went berserk. The onlookers from the town, who had gathered to watch the proceedings, began laughing at the whole event—not exactly the reaction the Klan wanted.

Finally, in frustration, the Klan gave up, packed up, and headed off for home. Our Love Night volunteers followed them to their cars, giving them red roses and heart-shaped balloons.

It's amazing that nobody got hurt. The cheerleaders were scared, and the local police did their best to reassure them that they would be protected (and they were). Some said that Georgia had not seen so much love since Newt left his first wife for a younger woman.

Love Night for the Aryan Nations

Each summer, the Nazis, neo-Nazis, Aryans, Klan, and skinheads put aside their differences and come together in the beautiful mountains of Idaho for their annual convention. It's a virtual pot-

The Aryans turn their backs on love.

pourri of hate. Here, they share ideas and strategies and try out the latest techniques in cross burning.

We discussed a variety of ways to deliver them a big dose of *TV Nation* love. At first we thought of doing an airdrop of love notes over the Aryan compound. Nineteen pilots in the area turned us down. One man said he'd do it—until he spotted a tower with a sharpshooter in it.

We then turned to an idea we were sure would bring delight to the Nazis: a multiracial chorus line singing and dancing to the great Motown hit "Stop! In the Name of Love." Placing ourselves on the dirt road outside the compound, we cranked up the music, and the young women from a local dance company broke into a spirited dance number.

It wasn't long before the Aryans heard the commotion and headed down their driveway toward the dancers. The women kept on going as the Nazis got closer and closer. The police were nowhere in sight, and we discovered that the security guards we hired had, against our wishes, brought guns. It was very tense.

The Love Night Dancers.

The Nazis who were in uniform stayed on their side of the road giving the Love Night dancers a raised hand and a "Sieg heil!" The skinheads, though, weren't so formal. They crossed the road and headbutted the camera. The women kept dancing. The skinheads got angrier. At that moment the police arrived and the potential for violence was averted.

Love Night for Operation Rescue

Each week throughout the country, members of Operation Rescue show up at abortion clinics and harass women who are on their way inside for help. They shout "baby killer" and "murderer" at them. They take photographs. They shove grotesque photos of aborted fetuses in their faces.

Lately, these hate peddlers have begun showing up at the homes of doctors and clinic workers. They harass their spouses and children. The extreme wing of the antiabortion movement has assassinated doctors who run clinics. In 1997, abortion clinics in the United States experienced 166 "incidents of violence" that included seven arsons, eleven death threats, six assaults, sixty-two stalkings, sixty-five cases of vandalism, and one attempted murder.

This is probably the most successful hate movement in the country. Even though abortion has been legal for over twenty-five years, these right-to-life individuals have put such fear into people who run the clinics that today 84 percent of all the counties in the country have no doctor, hospital, or clinic that will perform an abortion.

On Love Night, we turned the tables and went to visit the head of Operation Rescue West at his home in the mountains outside Los Angeles. When the *TV Nation* volunteers arrived, instead of

The *TV Nation* Love Squad visits the Right-to-Lifers.

shouting at him, they offered to plant flowers and shrubs in his yard. He came out of the house and was not amused. In a move that was not exactly pro-life, he angrily stomped on some of the flowers until they were smashed into the ground.

After trying to insult our crew with various remarks about "feminists," he gave up and went inside. We replanted the flower bed he destroyed and then went on our merry way.

Love Night for Jesse Helms

Jesse Helms, the U.S. senator from North Carolina, has led the fight against gay rights for years. Even bills to help people with AIDS are opposed by this man, who loves to describe in graphic detail on the floor of the Senate what it is that gay men like to do. Likes to describe it a little too much.

Because we believed Jesse needed a little lovin' from his fellow man, we decided to form the *TV Nation* Gay Men's Chorus. We rented a bus and headed down to Washington, D.C. Standing on the corner of 1st Street and Constitution Avenue (the Dirksen Building),

The TV Nation Gay Men's Chorus serenades Senator Jesse Helms.

our choir began serenading Senator Helms outside his office window with a rendition of "What the World Needs Now Is Love." Soon, the Capitol police showed up to put a halt to the singing.

"It's against the law to sing on Capitol Hill," one told us. "You'll need a permit."

With that we headed off to Arlington, Virginia, where Helms lives. Striding down the sidewalk in front of his house, the *TV Nation* Gay Men's Chorus sang "On the Street Where You Live."

The door to Helms's house opened and out came his wife. She seemed quite surprised and pleased. She thanked the choir and told them she was sorry the senator wasn't home.

We were too.

Love Night was one of the most difficult pieces for us to get on the air. Executives at the Fox Network feared that even mentioning these groups would give them more publicity than they deserved. Others worried that the confrontational nature of the segment would result in harassment no one wanted.

But more than that, the feeling was that no advertiser would want its product anywhere near this piece. We went back and forth with the network's Standards and Practices department, fighting for Love Night. It had become a personal favorite of most of the *TV Nation* crew. In the end, the network said that each segment could run except the one on abortion (we had been told by both networks not to do any stories on abortion). We were asked to "eliminate two of the five swastikas" in the Nazi segment and to audibly mask "one of the three times the word 'gook' is mentioned." Instead you hear a dog bark.

The day before Love Night was to air, the entire length of the show came up two minutes short. We suggested that the only way to solve the problem was to run the two-minute abortion segment. The network gave in but only after we significantly softened the piece and added the words "These extremist acts have been disavowed by the mainstream Right-to-Life movement."

3

Invading the Beach at Greenwich, Connecticut

Imagine if one day the voters of Arizona declared that from now on, only the legal residents of the state of Arizona would be allowed to visit the Grand Canyon. What if Brooklyn mandated that only Brooklynites could go to Coney Island? What would happen if the state of Mississippi said that no boat other than those owned by the citizens of Mississippi could use the Mississippi River?

The people living in the rest of the country wouldn't put up with it. As Americans, we have this belief that huge tracts of national parks, forests, and coastlines are the property of all the people and no private individual can "own" them.

It appears, though, that some communities would prefer to keep these natural wonders all to themselves. Throughout the nation, a number of wealthy, white towns have instituted measures to keep "other people" out of their neighborhoods.

Take Greenwich, Connecticut. One of the richest communities in America (according to the *New York Times,* the average selling price of a home here is over $1.1 million), Greenwich is the toniest of all the New York City suburbs. The boyhood home of former president George Bush, Greenwich is nearly all white, and some of America's richest families and CEOs live there.

When you've got it this good, you tend to want to keep it. Too bad that this country is built on the principle of "liberty and justice for all." That really gets in the way of having a good time!

One day in 1994, a young man from nearby Stamford, Connecticut, Brenden Leydon, was running along the beaches of Long Island Sound when he crossed the town line of Greenwich. Jogging onto the beach at Greenwich Point, he was stopped by a guard and asked to show his "resident's beach card." Brenden asked, "What's that?" The guard told him that only legal residents of Greenwich could use the beach and they had to have a resident's card to prove it.

Leydon wanted to know if this was a private beach. No, he was told, this is a public beach—but just for the public of Greenwich. Yes, it is operated with tax dollars, but only from the taxes of Greenwich. Therefore it is just for the well-heeled people of Greenwich.

Much to Greenwich's bad luck, Leydon also happened to be a third-year law student at Rutgers University. He filed suit against Greenwich and the town gave him a temporary beach pass allowing him to use the beach until the case went to trial and a judge decided whether the all-white, all-rich beaches of Greenwich should be open to all Americans.

We were short a story for an upcoming episode of *TV Nation,* so when the morning's paper arrived with the news of Leydon's suit, we instantly knew that *TV Nation* had to pay a visit to Greenwich, Connecticut.

The problem was, we had only four days to prep, produce, and shoot the piece. We would then have only another five days to edit it. This entire process, for a typical story on *TV Nation,* usually took about three to five weeks. But the possibility of giving the good people of Greenwich a dose of reality was too great an opportunity to let slip by.

It was decided that we would liberate the beaches of Connecticut. We would gather a group of people from the streets of New York City, hire a bus, and head for a day of fun in the sun.

We also felt that this would be a perfect job for our occasional guest correspondent, Janeane Garofalo. She enthusiastically agreed to do it.

As background for the piece, we sent a crew ahead a day early to interview townsfolk about the city ordinance. Everyone we spoke to supported the beach ban. They talked of "hordes" of people coming from "everywhere" if their beaches were open. ("Where would we put everyone?") One man reassured us that the rich are

Janeane Garofalo: before the invasion.

very kind to minorities: "Look how many we hire to clean our homes!"

Within seventy-two hours, the producers had arranged the largest beach invasion since Normandy. Helicopters, planes, boats, buses, the works. Off-duty police divers from New York City were hired to make sure no one drowned. The entire staff stopped working on the stories they were assigned and pitched in.

Then the shoe dropped. Our studio, Columbia TriStar, told us that we could not do the story because it would involve breaking the law.

"It's not 'the law,' " we told the studio's lawyer. "It's the law of *Greenwich, Connecticut!*"

We thought it out and found a way to satisfy Columbia TriStar. Public trust doctrine says that the federal government actually owns the water, if not the sand, along any coast. So, as long as we stayed below the high-tide mark on the beach, we were not technically on Greenwich property. Satisfied with this liberal interpretation of the law, the studio said "OK," and we were off.

On a sunny Saturday morning we gathered our rainbow beach coalition together and headed out of the city on our chartered bus. Because *TV Nation* was a union show, everyone had to be a member of the extras union. When we handed out the instructions for the day, many of the individuals became alarmed and chose not to go.

The instructions read, in part:

> *If the police decide to give you a ticket, please immediately bring your ticket to the producer. While it is extremely unlikely that the police will threaten any sort of arrest, please obey all police officers in this situation.*

You can understand why some people wouldn't want to stick with the shoot, especially if they were of a certain skin persuasion. A night in the Greenwich jail was not a perk of being on television.

But a good dozen of the extras decided to take the risk, and we set off for the beach. The bus turned off the highway and onto the road leading to the water. At the guard booth we were stopped and asked to show our resident's permit. Of course, all we had was our American citizenship, so the guard ordered the bus to turn around and sent us away.

There was a moan of disappointment all around, but Janeane kept the *TV Nation* crowd going with "Beach Party!" chants and told everyone that there was more than one way to get on that forbidden sand.

The bus headed off to a nearby marina. There, everyone boarded a large boat with a half-dozen smaller boats attached to it. With their beach balls, lawn chairs, and sunscreen lotion, the *TV Nation* armada, complete with helicopters overhead, pulled out of port and raced toward Greenwich.

Back at the beach, the happy people of Greenwich were enjoying the beautiful day when they looked up from their slumber and, all of a sudden, in what seemed like a scene out of *Apocalypse*

TV Nation citizens lead the armada
to the forbidden sands of Greenwich, Connecticut.

Now, they saw The People coming toward them at seventy-five knots.

It was a glorious sight. Janeane stood at the helm of the boat proudly holding the *TV Nation* flag, looking like George Washington crossing the Delaware. It appeared as if we were going to make it all the way to shore until . . .

Out of the south came a police boat at top speed. We tried to outrun them, but it was no use. They intercepted the boat and demanded to know what we were doing. We told them the truth—and they threatened us with arrest. At that point, a Coast Guard boat appeared upon the scene and we knew that the situation was now serious. (Though we were used to local police putting a halt to our activities, this marked the first time on *TV Nation* that a branch of the armed forces was called in.)

The Coast Guard officer was very aggressive in threatening action against us and demanded to come on board. As she was stepping over to our boat, she slipped and fell into the water. She was so embarrassed that we were sure we were going to feel the heat of her

Janeane and fellow TV Nation crew emerge from the sea on Greenwich Beach.

wrath. Instead, we fished her out of the ocean. She was grateful and toned down her threats considerably. She inspected the boat and found that it was in perfect condition and operating legally.

The police said we could not take even our smaller boats in any closer. After a short tactical discussion we asked, "Would it be OK if we swam to shore?" The police said that we were free to swim in the water, but we couldn't set foot on the Greenwich beach. So, inspired by the moment and determined to complete the quest, Janeane and the others leapt overboard and swam the half mile to shore.

By the time they arrived, the residents of Greenwich were outraged. They booed, screamed, and shouted at Janeane. "Go back to where you came from!"

"If you like it so much here, why don't you buy a house and own property and then you can use the beach!" one man yelled at her.

"Well, with such a friendly attitude like that, I can't wait to move here!" Janeane replied.

The beachgoers begged the police to have us arrested. But the producer, Joanne Doroshow, having worked out the legalities in advance (she and the crew had press permits to be on the beach), escorted Janeane

How to Get to Greenwich Beach, Greenwich, Connecticut

From New York City:

Get on I-95 heading north.

Get off at exit 5 in Connecticut.

At the end of the exit, turn right on Route 1 (you are now heading east).

Drive for a hundred yards or so until you come to a stoplight.

Turn right on Sound Beach Avenue.

Drive through Old Greenwich until you get to the shoreline.

Turn right on Shore Road—this will lead you right into the beach parking lot.

and the others along the high-tide mark to the end of the beach and then off the lot where the bus was parked.

The town threatened us with all kinds of legal action (including filing a complaint with the FAA over our use of the chopper), but nothing came of it because we had stayed within the "law."

The final arguments in Mr. Leydon's lawsuit against Greenwich were held in late March 1998. The *TV Nation* "Beaches" segment was played in court by Mr. Leydon to prove people who were trying to use the beach for free expression were not being allowed to do so. The tape was watched, but was not admitted as evidence. The judge ruled that because Greenwich does allow outsiders to enter the beach with a resident, the policy does not restrict freedom of expression. Greenwich residents claim their policy controls traffic and protects the beach's ecology.

Mr Leydon plans an appeal.

4

Payback Time

We are, as we all know, powerless.

We have little or no control over the events that shape our lives. We find ourselves at the mercy of our employer and the whims of the economy. Each day is a struggle to survive the beating we call a life. Nothing works—the roads, the phones, the postal service, AOL, HMOs, the self-service gasoline pump—and, with resignation, we accept it, like having to learn a new area code every month.

The computer you just bought is already so obsolete your nine-year-old is laughing hysterically at your inadequate RAM.

You're expected to be at work before the sun rises and you had better not leave before the sun sets or you may not see the sun rise over your miserable little cubicle tomorrow.

We no longer get a human when we call a business. ("Press 1 if you would like to hear a directory of what to press, press 2 if you don't mind being on hold for an hour . . .")

You have a vague memory of what a "savings" account used to be and you've figured out that the way to get through the next month is to sign up for *just one more* credit card—the one that came in the mail today at only 17 percent interest.

People you know in their forties are finding lumps in their brains—and they're the ones who haven't eaten meat or dairy in ten years!

The media assaults you with information you don't need and refuses to give you the goods on what you want to know. Just shut up and buy that new Jeep Cherokee they're shoving down your throat during a time-out in the Bulls game—a time-out *the network* has called because you haven't bought anything in the last six minutes! PICK UP THAT PHONE NOW, VISA AND MASTERCARD ACCEPTED.

Wouldn't you like to give them all a taste of their own medicine? Wouldn't you like to stick it to them without going postal? Aren't you more than mad as hell?

At *TV Nation,* we decided we weren't going to take it anymore.

Yep, it was payback time. Big payback time.

In the heart of Times Square we asked average citizens if they'd like to dish out some payback to those who were driving them crazy. We promised to go after anyone and everyone, no holds barred.

We called it "Payback Night."

The Car Alarm People

Who hasn't been awakened at three in the morning by one of those deafening, obnoxious car alarms that go off for no apparent reason? What is the point of those things? Have YOU ever called the police when you've heard those alarms go off? Of course you haven't! No one has! Honestly, no one! We asked the cops how many times they get calls from a concerned citizen when a car alarm goes off.

"Never," was their reply. They explained that the only calls they get are from neighbors "asking us to come over and shoot the damn thing dead."

We decided to go to the home of the CEO of Audiovox, the largest car alarm company in the country. There, in an exclusive neighborhood just outside New York City, we parked a dozen cars along the secluded drive to his house, and, at six in the morning, we let those babies rip. Wang! Wang! Wha! Wha! WOOOO! WOOOO! Beep! Beep! They played their tunes like a bad jazz band in a large stadium. But it was a symphony to our ears as we watched the chairman come out of the house in his jammies.

A familiar sight through the lens of the TV Nation cameras.

He was so upset he called the cops. When they arrived they threatened us with arrest for disturbing the peace. "What about the peace of millions of Americans who are disturbed by this guy?" we asked. The officer tried to control his own glee at seeing this captain of industry being given a little payback.

The officer asked us to turn off the alarms. "That's the beauty of the things, sir," our producer replied. "They go on and on and on for a good five minutes. You just can't turn them off."

The alarms died out and we left. Later, the CEO called the network and threatened to sue. After much negotiation—and a refusal on our part to edit the piece—it aired intact, with only one concession: we promised not to tell the viewing audience where he lived.

Telemarketers

Is there anything more annoying than total strangers calling you at eight o'clock at night trying to get you to switch to MCI or buy a new insurance policy? OK, an evening with Rush Limbaugh in your living room would be more annoying. But other than that, is there anything that ticks you off more than telemarketing companies?

We found the home phone number of the CEO of one of the largest telemarketing firms in the country and decided to see how he liked it. Over and over again, *TV Nation* staffer Gideon Evans called this man asking him if he "had heard of a new and exciting television show that is—get this—ABSOLUTELY FREE! It's called *TV Nation!*"

Gideon Evans annoys the hell out of a telemarketing CEO.

At first, the telemarketing guru just hung up. But as Gideon kept calling back, the CEO got more and more perturbed. He started quoting various telemarketing laws that prohibit such companies from harassing people.

Well, in our collective mind, we figured, "Wouldn't that be EVERY telemarketing call?" He threatened to call the police. We all thought that was a great idea and we now encourage everyone to tell the telemarketer, "Look, I know you're only doing your job, but I've got a trace on this call and I'm dialing the police right now to have your boss arrested."

Dumpster Trucks

Following car alarms as the single biggest reason we can't get enough sleep at night is garbage and Dumpster trucks. We have nothing against garbage men. They certainly have one of the lousiest jobs on the planet.

But the invention of the Dumpster has taken things beyond the pale. The way they are designed to operate—the loud clang, lift, and bang to the ground and the beep, beep, beep when they are in reverse—makes for frightening sounds to wake to at 2:00 A.M. In addition, if the Dumpster doesn't land back in exactly the right spot, it must be lifted and banged down again.

There has to be a better way. Instead of intellectuals in think tanks at places like Stanford sitting around dreaming up new methods of war, can't they devise a more aesthetically pleasing, environmentally friendly way of collecting large amounts of refuse?

We couldn't wait for that day to come, so we took matters into our own hands. We hired a garbage/Dumpster truck to go with us at two in the morning to the homes of those who own these garbage companies (not all cities collect the garbage with public employees).

The only problem with this is that in the New York area where we were filming, some of the garbage companies are reputed to be mob related. This was a huge concern for us. At the

first home, as we started our lifting and banging, a woman came out of the house and told us her husband had just left her for a younger woman and she was ready to spill the beans to us about every shady deal this guy had. We said, "Hey, we're not *60 Minutes,*" and left.

The next stop was at the home of a garbage king in New Jersey. As we began banging our Dumpster outside his window, he bolted out of the house and started after our cameraman. The producer wisely decided that this was not a safe situation and immediately packed up the gear and left. About a mile down the road the crew

A Taste of Their Own Medicine

Do you have any ideas for those who deserve a taste of their own medicine? Here are a few we didn't try:

- We set speed traps for police and pull them over.
- We go to the home of a person in charge of highways and do roadwork in his driveway so he can't move his car.
- We invite bouncers to a new club that they can't get into.
- We get into the home of the head of PBS and hassle him for donations.
- We run a jackhammer in front of the home of the person that invented the jackhammer.
- We intersperse canned laughter into a video we make of the life story of the inventor/CEO of canned laughter.
- We screw up the credit history of a record-club CEO.

pulled into a parking lot to regroup. All of a sudden, a van turned into the lot and a bunch of big guys in their boxers and slippers (including the garbage king we had just filmed) hopped out and formed a circle around the crew. This, by the way, is the universal sign that you are about to get your ass kicked.

Our producer told them that this was all for an innocent little comedy piece and we didn't want to donate any blood in the name of a twenty share on Fox. It turned out that the man's father had been killed in a mob hit the previous year and they all thought we might be part of some other Mafia action. Since when did the Mafia start filming their hits?

The crew gingerly returned to their cars and escaped without a scratch. It took a few hours for everyone's nerves to calm down.

Jehovah's Witnesses

After that near-death experience, we decided to pick only on groups committed to pacifism, but with the criterion of still being really annoying.

Of course, that could only be the Jehovah's Witnesses. The Jehovah's Witnesses are the religious people who knock on your door and try to convert you. They want you to ask them in so they can bring you the Good News. They are so clean and nice and polite it is virtually impossible to get rid of them.

We did some research and got a list of where members of Jehovah's Witnesses lived and Mike went and knocked on their doors.

"Good morning!" Mike announced. "I've come to you with Good News! May I come into your house and share with you the story about a TV show which has changed my life and can change yours too?"

To the Jehovahs' credit, they immediately got the point and the joke. But they didn't promise to quit wearing those white shirts and ties and showing up on our doorstep at inopportune times.

The Hotel That Wants You Out by 11:00 A.M.

If you've ever stayed in a hotel, you know that checkout time is usually by noon, sometimes earlier. They want you out as soon as possible so they can get new customers into the room.

One way they like to nudge you out the door before you're ready to go is to have the maid unlock your door and barge in to clean the place. You are usually naked, and often you might be doing that thing which naked people do when there are two of them. The maid says, "Oh, I'm sorry!", shuts the door, and goes somewhere to write down what she just witnessed so she can send it to the Special Prosecutor.

The TV Nation housekeeper barges in.

We wondered if the heads of the Hilton Hotels or the Hyatt or Marriott have ever had their employees just waltz right in on them early in the morning. So we hired a maid, located Mr. Barron W. Hilton's mansion near Bel Air, California, and tried to pay him a visit—cleaning cart and all—well before "checkout" time.

One fine California morning, the *TV Nation* housekeeper merrily rolled her cart up Hilton's driveway and announced at the gate that she was "here to make his bed, fold the end of the toilet paper into a triangle, and provide clean towels." To our astonishment, the gate was opened and they let her in. But by the time they opened the door to the house, someone had figured out what was going on and finally sent her away, miniature *TV Nation* shampoo bottles and all.

Muzak

Everywhere you go, it's there. The 101 Strings versions of "Stairway to Heaven," "The Bitch Is Back," and "Revolution." To many, it's like nails on a blackboard. But there is no way to avoid it.

We will rock you (lightly).

We wondered, does the head of Muzak, Inc., have to listen to his own stuff? Probably not. So we thought he should have to face the music. We drove a flatbed trailer loaded with concert-sized speakers, followed the map to his home, parked the mega-amps, and cranked the Muzak up to "11."

Unfortunately the chairman wasn't home, but the neighbors were and they called the police, who, as they often did on *TV Nation*, showed up to shut us down—or else. We don't like "or else," so we packed up the truck, rewound the tape of Black Sabbath as performed by the London Symphony, and left.

Payback Night was complete.

5

The Corp-Aid Concert

After eight NBC episodes, it became clear to much of our audience that we at *TV Nation* had a problem with the way corporations run this country. Week after week, we would visit corporate giants and cause a bit of havoc—if not in their boardrooms, then at least in their lobbies.

When it came time to do a year-end special during Christmas week 1994, we thought that in keeping with the spirit of the season, we should be kind and try to do something nice for those businesses we had so maligned.

We received a letter from a fan who had an idea for *TV Nation*. "Are you aware," he asked, "that companies have no mechanism through which to receive gifts? There is no system to accept a donation from a well-wisher. Businesses are set up to sell products or services which in turn give them income. If they are a public corporation, they sell stock as a means to raise capital. They can also seek investors who are promised a certain profit for every dollar they invest should the company succeed.

"But if an average Joe just wanted to write AT&T a check one morning and slip it in the mail with a little note saying, 'Here, this is for you, just because you're YOU!', he would probably have the check returned since there exists no bookkeeping procedure for accepting cash contributions."

We decided to try out this theory and bring tidings of great joy to some of the country's most abused corporations.

We convinced NBC to give us a briefcase full of tens and twenties totalling $10,000. We then made a list (just like Santa) of who's been naughty and who's been caught. From that, we chose five companies that had been hit hardest with government fines (for pollution, price-fixing, hazardous working conditions, etc.) or judgments from lawsuits filed against them.

With the list in hand, Michael went off with the briefcase and attempted to hand over the ten grand to the first deserving corporation that would accept it.

The first stop was the Pfizer Corporation headquarters in New York City. Pfizer had just settled with claimants for $215 million for providing faulty artificial heart valves used in bypass operations. In addition, they paid the government a $10.75 million fine for submitting false statements to gain FDA approval of the valve. The defective devices cost hundreds of people their lives, and Pfizer was held accountable by the government and the relatives of the victims.

In addition to the cash, Mike was accompanied to Pfizer headquarters by a barbershop quartet singing Christmas carols for the executives and a tap dancer holding a big $10,000 check. (Check or cash, we had both.)

A vice-president of corporate communications came down to greet us—and to turn down the money. Sure enough, just as that *TV Nation* fan had predicted, the executive told us that "Pfizer has no means by which to accept a charitable contribution." He explained to us that they make money, they don't "take" it.

Then, he showed us the door.

Our next potential gift recipient was Prudential Securities, the insurance company. They were socked in 1994 with a $330 million fine for defrauding investors. They were well deserving of our gift—they had broken all previous records for a Wall Street crime.

The guard at the desk refused to let us take our gift to the chairman. He told us we were "crazy." Again, we were shown the door.

The *TV Nation* crew moved on to United Parcel Service (UPS). In 1994, UPS received the largest fine from the Occupational Safety and Health Administration (OSHA) for failing to improve the way in which their workers were handling packages that contained dangerous chemicals. We thought that maybe the check and the briefcase of cash weren't doing the trick, so this time we brought $10,000 in gold. The UPS public relations person thought the joke was pretty funny and played along until we started bringing up the OSHA fine. His mood changed rapidly and he walked away, shut the door to the offices behind him, and locked it.

Maybe he really did believe it was better to give than to receive.

Our Christmas journey next lead us to Kodak. Kodak had received huge fines for polluting the groundwater under residential communities with hazardous chemicals near their photo film factory in Rochester, New York.

This time, instead of being turned down by the security guard in the lobby and getting nowhere, we decided to follow the motto: "The path to truth is through the delivery entrance." And if you look like you're delivering something, you're in, no questions asked.

So we chose to use the back door to the Kodak building and found it quite easy to get to the floor where the executive offices were.

"How did you get in here?" they screamed. A couple of the men, apparently security, began to rough us up. They physically pushed us out the door, down the hall, and into the elevator (and rode down with us). We were then taken outside and told that they had called the police.

Despondent that no one would take his gift, Michael roamed up and down Wall Street with his briefcase wide open, appealing to anyone with an annual income of over $200,000 a year to step up, reach in, and grab himself some free cash.

No one did.

We had another idea. Why not throw a benefit concert for needy corporations—right in front of the New York Stock Exchange? Look at Live-Aid and its "We Are the World" song and how much that raised for charity. Or Farm-Aid, and how much that raised for hard-hit farmers.

So, why not "Corp-Aid"?

We rented a huge flatbed truck and placed it just down the block from the stock exchange. We asked the Meat

No takers for the briefcase o' cash.

We Are All Corporations

Words and Music by Jay Martel

We always hear people cry
About the little guy getting
    enough,
But who takes care of the big
    guy
When the going gets tough?

We take for granted the toil
Of bringing fuel to our cars.
Don't cry over spilled oil
We should be reaching for the
    stars, 'cause—

CHORUS:
We are all corporations
In our own way,
Makin' profits and gettin' fined,
It's the American way.

We all share the dream
Of getting really big and really
    rich.
It's time to forget the past
It's all just oil under the bridge.
'Cause the day is coming
You can feel it comin' round,
When the whole world over
Looks just like Prince Andrew
    Sound, 'cause—

We are all corporations
And it's time to say enough,
No more fines or regulations
Set us free to do our stuff.

Spoken interlude:
It's really great to be here and
sense the totally giving energy.
This is what Corp-Aid is all
about, man. Giving to the people
who take. The people in these
big buildings all around us: For
years they've been taking everything they can get their hands
on. And that's beautiful—that's
what the system is all about. But
in this last year, they've been hit
with some heavy fines, man. I'm
sorry, I always get a little emotional talking about this. They're
being forced to give something
up. Isn't it time we gave something back?

We are all corporations
In our own way,
Makin' profits and gettin'
    fined
It's the American way.

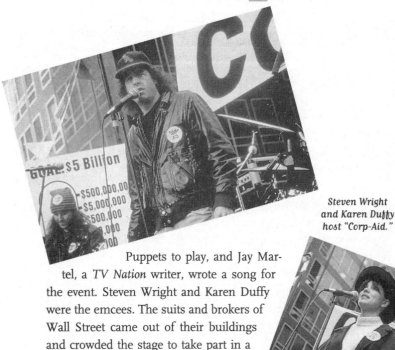

*Steven Wright
and Karen Duffy
host "Corp-Aid."*

Puppets to play, and Jay Mar-
tel, a *TV Nation* writer, wrote a song for
the event. Steven Wright and Karen Duffy
were the emcees. The suits and brokers of
Wall Street came out of their buildings
and crowded the stage to take part in a
history-making event. People wore
"Corp-Aid" stickers and swayed back
and forth listening to the music.
There were a lot of police. *TV
Nation* staffers passed buckets
throughout the crowd. We told everyone that all the money raised that day would go
to help Exxon pay off the huge judgment they got over the
Exxon *Valdez* accident, which spilled millions of gallons of oil along
the Alaskan coast.

The Meat Puppets kicked into the "Corp-Aid" anthem and the
crowd reached deep into their pockets. Don't ever say the wealthy
don't give. When we counted the money at the end of the concert,
we had received a whopping $275.64 to give to Exxon.

The next week, Mike flew down to Dallas to present the bucket o'
cash, as we named it, to the chairman of Exxon. Unfortunately, even

though Mike had gone to all the bother of traveling to Texas, the guard and the PR people would not let him near the chairman's office. They wouldn't even accept his gift. They DID accept a free copy of a book he gave to them: *When Bad Things Happen to Good People*. It was a start.

As Mike left, he placed the bucket on the lawn with the hopes that someone from Exxon would come out and accept his yuletide offering.

As the crew drove away, they saw that someone did.

The groundskeeper.

"*Feliz Navidad!*" they shouted out the window as they waved good-bye.

The Meat Puppets sing our anthem.

Mike collects cash for Exxon from a charitable Wall Street broker.

6

Crackers, the Corporate Crime-Fighting Chicken

"Why did the chicken cross the road?
To kick some CORPORATE ASS! That's why!"

Sometimes, when all else fails, you need to call in a Superhero.

When forest fires are out of control, you need Smokey the Bear.

When polluters threaten our environment, you call in Woodsy Owl ("Give a hoot! Don't Pollute!").

When crime is running rampant, who else is there "to take a bite out of crime" but McGruff, the Crime Dog.

But what does one do when the threat is from an entity so evil, so malevolent, that it seems no human being has the power to stop it?

Handmade sign from a fan.

Yes, we're talking about Corporate Criminals, those men in suits who flagrantly violate the law and bring harm to the world. They run amok across the planet, with the rest of us mere mortals unable to subdue them.

Each year in America, we lose $4 billion to burglary and robbery, but we lose $200 billion due to corporate fraud. And each year, forty-five thousand more people lose their lives due to corporate workplace hazards than those who are murdered by handguns.

The list goes on and on—and yet, nothing is said or done about it. No eleven o'clock newscasts opening with the latest death on the job, or the hiring of more police to patrol Wall Street and nab the white-collar crook.

We at *TV Nation* felt that the country deserved better. If the street criminals had an animal mascot chasing them, then why not the corporate criminals?

Thus was born Crackers, the Corporate Crime-Fighting Chicken.

Crackers became the first primetime Superhero to go after the very people who might be advertising on the Superhero's show. This paradox was not lost upon the network—they did not welcome the Chicken with open arms. But they withheld judgment until they saw the chicken in action.

The evolution of Crackers.

Crackers was a seven-foot chicken. (Though some claimed it was just a costume worn by one of our writers, John Derevlany, those of us who believed knew that the Chicken was real and would save us from Evil.) We gave him special powers to investigate wrongdoing and ask the tough questions of Big Business that the press is afraid to ask.

The Corporate Crimemobile.

We provided Crackers with his own Crimemobile, a long trailer with a lab, computers, and handcuffs. His mission was to travel across the country in this Crimemobile, listening to the concerns of average citizens who were victims of the decisions made by businesses and their officers. Crackers also had his own toll-free 800 number that people could call to report corporate crimes in progress. Over forty thousand calls were received the first weekend.

That alone made Crackers a worthy creation. The number of calls from average citizens who had real examples of wrongdoing at the places where they worked or lived was astounding. We were in awe of the broad scope of criminal behavior of those who, as Woody Guthrie said, rob you with a pen instead of a gun.

We sent Crackers off on his journey, visiting towns and corporations in over a dozen cities. This Chicken had enough material for his own show, but we had time to present only five of his crime-fighting accomplishments.

New York: First Boston Corp.

First Boston, one of the country's largest financial institutions, had gone to the mayor of New York for a tax break. They were threatening to leave the city if their taxes were not reduced.

Was this "extortion"? That would have been grounds enough for Crackers to go after First Boston. Though human society did not consider this *illegal* extortion, Crackers found it a prime example of how companies stick up communities for large sums of money, always under the threat that something bad will happen to the community when they pull out. Fearing the worst, virtually every town gives in.

In January 1995, First Boston got their multimillion-dollar tax break and added it to their annual coffers. And, within thirty days of receiving this "gift" from the taxpayers of New York, what did First Boston do? They laid off over a hundred people. Just like that.

Ironically, part of their deal with the city was that they were going to keep jobs in the city, not eliminate them. So did First Boston give the money back to the city after they broke the agreement?

Are you kidding?

Hundreds of fans turned out in Chicago to see the chicken.

Crackers was appalled and in no mood to kid around. He headed over to First Boston's headquarters near Madison Avenue to demand they reinstate the people or return the money to the city.

As soon as Crackers entered the doors of First Boston, he was confronted by security. But, unlike the mortal *TV Nation* correspondents (when rebuffed at corporate headquarters), the Chicken could not be stopped by men in rented uniforms. Crackers bolted through the guards, got on the escalator, and rode to the second floor. There he was met by even more security. These men seemed to have had some training in dealing with Superhero chickens because they were able to return Crackers back down the escalator to the first floor.

The New York police were called, and they showed up with a paddy wagon. Once on the scene, they realized they had brought the wrong paddy wagon—the one for humans. There was no way a seven-foot chicken was going to fit in that van.

So the cops decided to try and talk the Chicken out of the building. Crackers was happy to see his crime-fighting brothers and encouraged them to join him in confronting the officials of First Boston. But the cops said Crackers could go to City Hall and take it up with the mayor.

And that's exactly what the Chicken did.

Mayor Rudolph Giuliani was set to hold his daily press briefing that afternoon. When his aides alerted him that Crackers was just outside the pressroom (and Mike inside), he huddled with them for nearly an hour as they tried to figure out how to handle the situation. A reporter from WABC, friendly to the administration, tipped them off as to why Crackers was there. When Giuliani finally appeared at the podium, his aides and undercover police officers kept the Chicken outside the room and surrounded Mike inside it. Then the friendly reporter decided to steal the Chicken's thunder and asked the mayor about how tax breaks to companies like First Boston had helped to improve the city. Giuliani went on and on explaining how tax abatements made New York a more attractive place to do business.

Mike finally broke in and asked the mayor why he was refusing to face the crime-fighting chicken. The mayor responded, "I am not talking to a chicken." Crackers, watching through the window, seemed hurt by the rejection. This chicken is one sensitive bird. The mayor refused to bring charges against First Boston. Crackers couldn't get near the First Boston executives. It appeared that the Chicken had been dealt his first defeat. Sometimes the bad guys do win.

Brooklyn: Delta Enterprise Corp.

Crackers moved on to his next target—the Delta Enterprise company of Brooklyn, which makes baby walkers, those devices by which a baby can move around the room before it can walk on its own. The problem with many baby walkers is that the wheel bases aren't wide enough and babies can accidentally tumble down a flight of stairs. In 1997 alone, an estimated fourteen thousand babies required hospital emergency room treatment due to baby-walker-related injuries. Thirty-four deaths have been blamed on walkers since 1973.

Crackers showed up at the company's main factory and demanded to see the boss. Again, the Chicken was physically removed.

"Outta here! Outta here!" the man kept shouting.

Crackers then initiated a campaign to warn parents that the walkers can be unsafe. He convinced a number of moms and dads to turn in their walkers to him. In 1997, Delta Enterprise started making walkers that meet new safety standards determined by the Juvenile Products Manufacturers Association. Crackers joins Federal consumer safety officials urging parents to purchase walkers that meet these standards.

Philadelphia: Bounced Check Fees

Crackers wheeled his Crimemobile into downtown Philadelphia to the cheers of hundreds of Philadelphians. They had come to tell the Chicken about all the corporate crimes they had witnessed. But one infraction irked Crackers the most.

In 1995, CoreStates Bank was charging its customers $25 for every check they bounced. Currently the fee is $30. For families living from paycheck to paycheck, this is an extraordinary sum of money. Philadelphia has the highest fee in the country for bounced checks.

Banks across the nation rake in $4 billion in yearly profits from check overcharge fees alone.

Bouncing a check is not what it used to be. Writing a check for money you don't have in your account is itself illegal. But most citizens are law-abiding people and have no intention of ever bouncing a check. So the bank sets you up for the overcharge.

Here's how it works:

You deposit your paycheck on Friday, then go home and write a few checks to pay some bills over the weekend. But the bank puts a hold on your paycheck to make sure your employer's bank covers it. The hold could last ten days. Meanwhile, those checks you wrote—oh, your bank has quickly cleared those. You wrote those checks based on a balance you thought you had, one that included that paycheck. But the paycheck hasn't cleared, so . . . boinnnnggg! Bounced! And you're out another $30.

This practice is common all over America. It seems like theft to us. Yet no cop goes in and arrests the bank chairmen for theft.

Enter Crackers.

Crackers went to a Core-States bank and insisted the manager stop charging these incredible fees. The manager

Crackers leads the march to CoreStates Bank.

claimed she had no authority, that she was just doing her job. Crackers went to CoreStates headquarters and was turned away.

Fed up with not being taken seriously, the Chicken went to see State Representative Babette Josephs, who promised to introduce a bill in the Pennsylvania legislature prohibiting any bank from charging more than $7.50 for a bounced check and strictly defining what a bounced check is.

This was something that hit home with a lot of viewers, and Crackers got tons of mail from people who saw this story.

St. Louis: Doe Run Lead Pollution

We started announcing upcoming Crackers tour stops on *TV Nation*, and when Crackers arrived in that particular town, a crowd or a rally would be there to meet him. At a gathering in St. Louis, Crackers received a tip about a facility in a residential area called Herculaneum, just southeast of the city. The whistle-blower told Crackers that the townspeople felt that their community was being poisoned by the Doe Run lead factory, one of the largest lead operations in the world. Crackers decided to research the tip, and through talking to local residents and workers, he confirmed it.

Crackers then went about his business. He tried to enter the factory to confront the bosses but as usual was stopped by a police officer. (Later that day, the same cop pulled up alongside Crackers and asked to get his picture taken. It turns out he had watched the entire season of the show and loved the chicken.)

Crackers personally scooped his own soil samples and took them to a lab in St. Louis. The samples showed that the lead level was high. He had children tested for lead poisoning and found out that their blood had unacceptably high levels of lead. He had a meeting with the CEO of Doe Run. He contacted the Missouri Department of Natural Resources and was told that Doe Run was not in compliance with federal air-quality standards, although they are now following a state-monitored plan to cut emissions.

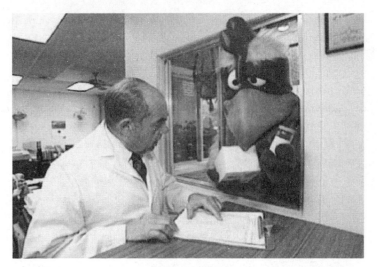

Crackers visits the lab.

After the show aired, two class-action suits were filed, one for property damage and one for personal injury. The Department of Natural Resources received between six hundred and seven hundred letters, and since Crackers brought attention to the situation on *TV Nation,* there is a greater awareness in the area about the dangers of lead.

Detroit: The Newspaper Strike

There are corporate crimes and then there are corporate crimes that are personal. The one that held special interest for us happened in our own backyard—the newspaper strike in Detroit, Michigan. Because we gave birth, so to speak, to Crackers, we made him an honorary Michigander.

The workers at the *Detroit Free Press* and *Detroit News* had gone out on strike in July of 1995 over a contract dispute. Management at both papers immediately hired scabs to produce the papers. Violent demonstrations resulted, with the police inflicting most of the violence.

By the time Crackers arrived, the workers had been on strike for over thirty days. The National Labor Relations Board (NLRB) had ruled against the newspapers, but management filed an appeal instead of coming to terms with the strikers. Crackers tried to act as a mediator but was ignored by management. He then went to see Congressman John Conyers, the top-ranking Democrat on the House Judiciary Committee. Conyers promised Crackers that he would hold hearings to help the workers get their jobs back and he would investigate ways to amend the antitrust laws, which permit two newspapers in a town to conduct business under a Joint Operating Agreement.

Next, Crackers decided to put out his own newspaper—at a union print shop—to tell the people of Detroit the truth about what management was doing to the workers. He even tried to deliver his paper to the homes of the publishers of the *Free Press* and *News*.

Finally, it was time for Crackers to take direct action. He led a group of strikers in a march on the two newspapers. The doors were immediately locked when security saw the big bird coming. Using

Crackers delivers the truth.

powers none of us had seen before, Crackers, with his bare wings, pried open the main doors of the *Detroit Free Press*. The security guards were in shock. They called for the police. The crowd shouted louder, "Let the Chicken in!" The police arrived and asked Crackers to take the demonstration elsewhere.

So he did—one block down the street, to the *Detroit News*. There, Crackers saw that the loading-dock doors were open, so he just walked right in. Rent-a-cops appeared immediately and, in unison, picked Crackers up and threw him back out onto the street—a good ten feet away. It was the first time any of us had seen a chicken fly. Inspired by this miracle, the crowd surged against the now-closing metal doors. A riot ensued. Punches were thrown. Billy clubs were swinging everywhere. The doors were demolished. Both our cameraman and sound

Crackers and Michael Moore lead the march through Detroit.

A Letter from Crackers

August 1995

Greetings Crimefighters,

I've been on the road for the past few weeks, winging it across America in search of corporate wrongdoing. I was sticking my big spongy orange beak in the face of some polluters in St. Louis. I was in Detroit, trying to break up the big American media monopolies (don't be surprised if we have trouble getting this one on the air). Even by chicken standards, Detroit was a tough town. I was physically thrown 10 feet by security at the site of the local newspaper strike. Yee-ow! That smarts! I'm a chicken. I'm not supposed to fly.

I also stopped in a whole bunch of other cities this past month—Indianapolis, Milwaukee, Chicago, Cincinnati, Cleveland, Pittsburgh, and Decatur, Illinois. I met anywhere from a few hundred to several thousand people in each city—all of them with killer corporate crime tips. In Chicago, where we had about 3,000 people, the crowd was so enthusiastic in its anti-corporate fervor, the city actually called in riot police to shut us down. My chicken sense was telling me to say "Braackk, the cops!" But alas, I am protected by several layers of feathers, foam, and metal—to say nothing of my giblets of steel—while the rest of you only have a few layers of skin to stop those baton blows. I cut my Chicago visit short.

For now, my corporate crime-gathering road trip is on hold until we find out where *TV Nation* will air next. In the meantime, keep fighting for Truth, Justice, and a little thing called Corporate Responsibility.

I am chicken. Hear me Braack. BRAACCKKKKK!

Send Crackers E-mail at:
Wingit9@aol.com

recordist were bruised and bleeding. Hey, this is a comedy show, for chrissakes! If Rupert Murdoch could only see us now!

The police again moved in and quelled the disturbance. No one was arrested, and we all scooted out of there with the footage.

Later that night, to cheer Crackers up (he actually required a visit to the hospital), we took him to Tiger Stadium where Mike was singing the Canadian national anthem before the baseball game with the Blue Jays (as part of our "Canada Night" salute

CRACKERS IS COMING TO YOUR TOWN!

for another episode). During the game, Crackers got to meet the Tigers' mascot and trade tales. (It was during this meeting that Crackers learned the other mascots had cooling systems inside their heads and he was soon demanding one for himself.) Kids attending the game all ran up to Crackers for an autograph, which he was more than happy to give. Any week Crackers was on *TV Nation*, our ratings with two- to eleven-year-olds were the second highest for all shows in our time slot.

Soon, the Crackers tour was over and the chicken retired to the Colonel Sanders Museum in Kentucky, where he awaits his return to crime fighting. It had been a long, hot summer and we had learned much about what The Man was up to. It was clear that Americans needed a Superhero who could defend their interests and look after their well-being. Some people used to think that was the Democratic Party, but that's another story.

Crackers became the most loved, most watched, most requested part of *TV Nation*. This one chicken had struck a real chord with the public.

Someday, he will return.

7

The CEO Challenge

One night while watching the evening news we saw a story about the Japanese auto industry. Right there before our eyes was the chairman of Honda, Nobuhiko Kawamoto, with a rivet gun in his hands building a Honda on the assembly line! Then he was in the cafeteria eating lunch with the other workers on the line. At the end of the piece, he drove away in his year-old Honda Accord.

Coming from autoworker families like we do, growing up in the hometown of General Motors, it was a strange sight. We can guarantee you, as sure as the sky used to be blue, that the head of Buick has not been near a rivet gun since the internship stint he had to perform before graduating from General Motors Institute. (Now called Kettering University, this is an actual college in Flint that used to do nothing but train GM managers and engineers.)

In fact, most of the heads of American companies are in those jobs not because they know how to *make* things but because they knew somebody who knew somebody and they eventually proved they knew how to ride the bottom line. They are graduates of the Harvard Business School, not builders, inventors, or, God forbid, actual workers.

Maybe, we thought, this is why so much of what is "made" in this country is getting more and more inferior. The guy in charge doesn't have a clue about what the company is really making. And he rarely has to use it himself. (The head of GM gets a new car every three months, so he never has to bond with Mr. Goodwrench.)

Perhaps the most embarrassing example of this lack of know-how was on February 4, 1992, when the CEO of the country itself, George Herbert Walker Bush, was dumbfounded when he witnessed an electronic checkout line in progress. As the clerk ran the UPC code on the loaf of bread over the electronic eye, Bush stared in amazement. It was as if the Martian leaders had just shown him how they make their heads spin around in a 360-degree whirl.

We had no idea that the rich and powerful are that stupid. How did they get to where they're at in the first place? Why aren't *we* there?

So, we got to thinking, wouldn't it be interesting to see just how many CEOs could actually build—or, for that matter, even *use*—the very products they sell to the public?

Could the head of Safeway bag groceries?

Could the president of AT&T fix a downed power line?

Could Leona Helmsley change the sheets?

Thus was born the idea of the "CEO Challenge."

We began by making a list of corporations, their chairmen, and what we would ask them to do. We promised that any winner of the CEO Challenge would receive a gold-plated putter and putting green for his private use.

We started calling around and found it quite difficult to get these chairmen on the phone. If we were able to speak to an assistant or public relations person, we would explain very simply what we wanted the boss to do. They all thought we were nuts.

But, if you want to be taken seriously, even if you *are* nuts, you've got to put your concept in writing. A written request, for some reason, always gets a response. Once you've written the chairman a letter, *you* have started a paper trail that, someday, could come back to haunt an underling. Assistants always take a letter seriously.

Mike's letter read:

Dear Chairman,

If you're anything like me, in the past ten years of hoopla over Japanese acumen and "efficiency" you've never lost faith in plain old Yankee ingenuity. Likewise, you can probably imagine my surprise, which melted into dismay, but quickly went from there into defiance, when I read that many Japanese CEOs like those from Honda and Sony, can actually build their company's products. And now they're going around bragging that they are somehow more "connected" than American CEOs because they know how to fiddle with whatever their company makes.

I didn't believe it at first either. But my researchers, all Americans, have shown me the footage. Oh, it's true, all right.

You may remember me as the director of the documentary *Roger & Me*. Well, recently, I've begun work on a new prime time magazine show, *TV Nation*, which will air nationally on NBC and internationally on the BBC this summer. I know you'll want to respond to the gauntlet that's obviously being thrown to us by the Japanese, and we at *TV Nation* would like to help you. We're in a unique position to provide you the means of showing the Japanese—and the world—that you're just as "plugged into" your products as any country's CEOs are to theirs. If you'll allow me and a small camera crew into your office, or a nearby factory, assembly line, or laboratory, I know we can prove to the world that our CEOs are second to none.

I know you won't let the U.S.A. down. I look forward to meeting you. I remain,

Proudly American and Sincerely Yours,
Michael Moore, Citizen

We sent this letter to the chairman of Chemical Bank and asked him to operate an ATM machine. We asked the CEO of Hershey to make us a candy bar. We requested that the head of Estée Lauder give Mike a facial.

Needless to say, the letters were all met with a negative response.

We then followed up, telling a number of the companies that we would indeed show up on May 26, to personally ask the chairman to perform the job. With camera crew in tow, we were off.

First stop was the New York headquarters of IBM. For some reason the security personnel in the lobby would not allow us to enter, so we set up our props on the sidewalk. With his bullhorn, Mike looked straight up toward the penthouse floor and issued his challenge:

"LOUIS GERSTENER, CHAIRMAN OF IBM, COME DOWN AND FORMAT THIS COMPUTER DISK!"

There was no response. Mike continued the challenge.

"Do not be afraid. We come in peace."

Mike held up the golden putter Gerstener would win if he formatted the disk. Still no bite. He even tried flattery.

Mike challenges the CEO of IBM.

"We use only IBM and IBM-compatible computers. We despise Apple! Macintoshes are toys! They are not real computers!"

You would think that would have done the trick, but, alas, Mr. Gerstener would not come down.

Next, we went to the headquarters of Philip Morris, where we challenged the CEO, Michael Miles, to roll a cigarette. We brought with us a bowl of tobacco leaves, rolling papers, filters and "unspecified chemical additives." The guards became alarmed at our presence and locked all the doors to the building. For nearly an hour, no one at Philip Morris could leave or enter. We thought about all those smokers inside who legally couldn't smoke in there and badly needed to get outside to light one up. But we only thought about it for a second.

"Mr. Miles," Mike belted over the loudspeaker, "I know this sounds like a stupid question, but what exactly did Philip Morris die from?"

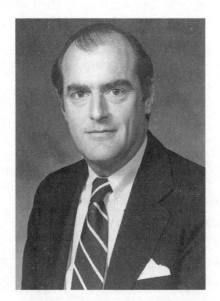

Michael Miles, CEO, Philip Morris.

Many passersby offered to roll a cigarette for us. Their speed and dexterity at this task was, to say the least, alarming. Mike continued his plea.

"Do not be afraid. I am unarmed. Please come down and explain the phrase, 'I'm a joker, I'm a smoker, I'm a midnight toker.'"

Mr. Miles, in the end, was a no-show.

We headed over to Park Avenue to the corporate offices of the Colgate-Palmolive Company to see if we could meet the boss, Reuben Mark. Rebuffed once again by the front desk, we set up shop on the sidewalk.

"Attention, attention! Mr. Reuben Mark, we need to know if you can do what your workers do. You are paid more than they are, and rightly so. We challenge you to come down and put the toothpaste in the tube."

Two hours went by and no Mr. Mark. We then took our appeal to his employees.

Reuben Mark, CEO, Colgate-Palmolive Company.

"People of Colgate-Palmolive: You all smell so good. Come out of the building so I can smell you up close."

A number of staff members actually came out to see us (and let us smell them). We tried to enlist their help in getting the chairman to come down and see us. They suggested that maybe the toothpaste in the tube thing was too difficult. Why not have him wash some dishes with a little Palmolive? Great idea, we thought. They went inside and soon came back out with the dish soap. We went and got some dishes, dirtied them up in a way only those who work on *TV Nation* could, and got a good suds going in the portable dishpan. The C-P workers then set about doing the dishes. Mike went back on the megaphone.

"Mr. Mark! We have met your employees and they can do the dishes! Can you?!"

Maybe it was the fear of dishpan hands, because Reuben Mark would not grace us with his presence.

We then got word from the Ford Motor Company that its CEO, Alex Trotman, would accept our challenge and change the oil in a Ford sports utility vehicle. Al Chambers, head of corporate communications for Ford, told us that while he thought it was a boring idea, his boss, Mr. Trotman, was "perfectly prepared to do what's asked of him, if they had some understanding as to why this would be 'visually interesting TV.' " We flew out to Detroit and went to the Ford proving grounds in nearby Dearborn. A garage was prepared and tools were organized in neat piles and ready to go for the challenge. Trotman drove up in his own car, got out, shook hands, and then got down to business. He parked a Ford Explorer onto two portable lifts. He drained the old oil, put new oil in, and changed the filter, all in under ten minutes! Autoworkers everywhere would now enjoy seeing the chairman on his back, with oil dripping all over him, doing the most manual of labor.

For his successful effort, Alex Trotman received the golden putter and putting green.

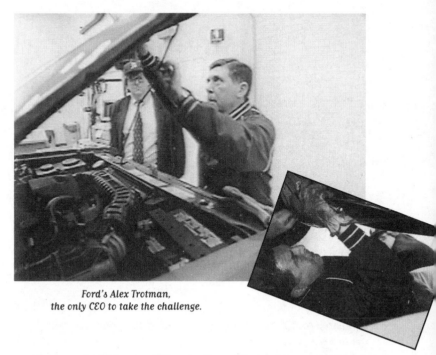

Ford's Alex Trotman,
the only CEO to take the challenge.

Trotman had his own TV crew there filming him. Later, Ford played the footage on monitors above assembly lines in every Ford plant in the world. Unlike the other chairmen who feared us (and feared we might pull some stunt to embarrass them), Trotman rightly took us at our word. He got a ton of mail and goodwill from those who watched the show.

It should be pointed out that Trotman is not an American. He is from Scotland and grew up in a system that believed that unions are a good thing and that companies must set an example of social responsibility. In 1997, when Johnson Controls, an auto-parts supplier to Ford, replaced its striking workers with scabs, Trotman refused to accept any parts from the company, causing him to lose two weeks' sales of his popular Ford Expedition model. Johnson Controls backed down and rehired its union workers.

Alex Trotman, CEO, Ford Motor Company.

This is not to say that Ford is not without its faults, but when compared to that company we grew up with in Flint . . . hey, don't get us started.

After we completed the story, we felt that, in the interests of fair play and full disclosure, there was still one CEO we had to challenge. Mike dutifully took his bullhorn out to the middle of Rockefeller Plaza.

"Jack Welch, chairman of General Electric, owner of NBC . . . PLEASE COME DOWN AND SCREW IN THIS LIGHTBULB!"

8

Brian Anthony Harris Is Not Wanted

There is one experience every African American male has had, and that is being stopped by the police for no reason at all. Whether it's because they're driving down the "wrong street" in the "wrong neighborhood," or they just "look suspicious," or the police are simply bored with nothing better to do, black men can regale you with tales of their close encounters with law enforcement when their only crime was going out to dinner.

The reason for this, as we all know, is that black guys are criminals.

And that's why we thought you might be interested in hearing the story of Brian Anthony Harris.

Brian is a young African American male who has been pulled over by the police somewhere between twenty and thirty times and accused of committing a crime. The only problem is, he's never so much as jaywalked across a street. Brian is a hardworking, church-going man who is director of lighting at Black Entertainment Television in Washington, D.C. He has a spotless record. That matters little to the D.C. police.

Time after time, the cops would pull Brian over to interrogate him for a recent murder, robbery, or assault. He would be yanked out of his car (a shiny BMW—a clear indication of his criminal activity), thrown to the ground, and held until one of them figured out he was the wrong guy.

After twenty or more incidents like this, anyone would get a little perturbed. We saw the story of Brian in a column by Colman McCarthy in the *Washington Post* and decided that Brian was in need of *TV Nation*. We called him up and asked if he would like our help in making sure the police never bothered him again. He was more than grateful for anything we could do.

What was needed was a campaign to dissuade the D.C. police from even *thinking* of pulling Brian over. With his assistance, *TV Nation* developed the following approaches:

- TV Ads

  TV Nation bought time on the local D.C. cable channel for ads imploring the police to stop harassing Brian. The thirty-second spot featured Brian speaking directly into the camera and politely pleading with the police to leave him alone.

- Billboards

  We rented billboards all over town—on buses and on roadsides—carrying the tag line "Brian Anthony Harris is NOT Wanted." We also had a mobile billboard mounted on a truck. We parked it across from various police precincts, drove it around Washington, and even took it for a spin by the White House.

Taking our message to The Man.

- Not Wanted Posters
  We made up some "NOT Wanted" posters and handbills with Brian's "mug shot" and his vital statistics, and asked local citizens, if they see this man, to tell the police to leave him alone! We stopped by the White House and left a stack to spread around there as well.

- Sky Messages
  We rented an airplane with a big banner trailing behind it and flew it over all precinct

NOT WANTED

FOR ANY CRIME

The above is a sketch resembling a suspect who is not wanted for anything. He has committed no crimes within the precincts of this city or any other city. This sketch is based on a description supplied by a witness.

DESCRIPTION: MALE, BLACK, CLEAR COMPLEXION, 30 YEARS OLD, 5' 10", 230 LBS, TRIMMED MUSTACHE & GOATEE, KNOWN TO SMILE

Male described above has been friendly and nice to most people he has met, and has never once caused harm to male or female victims. He abides by all laws of this and every other state, and would like to see others do the same. He is a good man. You'd probably like him if you met him.

However, Washington, D.C., Police have stopped him more than 20 times because of the way he looks. He's never been arrested. Just hassled a bit. We would like this to stop.

Notify the Special Stop Hassling Brian Harris Squad forthwith if you have any information relative to the subject. This case is being carried by TV Nation, which airs of Fox TV, channel 5, on Friday nights at 8.

TV NATION

Brian Anthony Harris and friend, Tyler Shives.

stations where Brian had been stopped. The banner read, "BRIAN ANTHONY HARRIS IS NOT WANTED."

- Other Stuff
  T-shirts were printed—one for Brian that read "I'm Not the Guy," and others for his friends that read "He Didn't Do It." Bumper stickers were placed on police squad cars that read, "I Brake for Brian Anthony Harris but I Don't Stop Him."

Once the city was inundated with the campaign to protect Brian Anthony Harris, it was time to take our case directly to The Man.

Brian and Michael walked into a police station, posted one of the "NOT Wanted" handbills, and asked to see the chief. They were shown the door. While this was happening, a policeman standing outside gave our billboard truck a parking ticket.

We do not give in easily at *TV Nation*, so we went on to another precinct. There we met a much friendlier sergeant who said he would speak to Brian about his problem—but only off camera. We

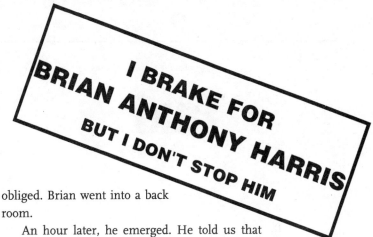

obliged. Brian went into a back room.

An hour later, he emerged. He told us that the cops had promised to stop harassing him. They gave him a special number to call if he ever gets pulled over. "They said just show this to any officer and he will leave me alone," Brian said.

Brian seemed pretty happy and very appreciative of our assistance. We checked back with him recently and he said that he has not been pulled over once since our broadcast. He said he is often recognized by cops on the beat and they get a big kick out of meeting him.

Well, we were glad we could help one African American man. But what about the millions of others who get harassed by the police?

At the end of the show the week we ran the Brian Anthony Harris segment, Mike offered some assistance for our African American male viewers. If they had been stopped by the police for no reason at all, they could call our 900 number and have their name placed on a large billboard that we would park in front of the FBI building in Washington, D.C. The billboard would ask the law-enforcement community of America to LEAVE THESE MEN ALONE!

The phones rang off the hook.

9

Taxi

Don't you miss the good ol' days, when racism wasn't all hidden and gussied up? The bathrooms were clearly marked "Whites Only" or "Coloreds." So were the drinking fountains, the waiting rooms, the bus and train seats, and, most importantly, the schools. Kind of gave us all a secure feeling, knowing who belonged and who didn't. Simple signs. Simple minds.

Then, in the 1950s and '60s, a bunch of do-gooders stuck their noses into the whole thing and upset the apple cart. No longer were the races to be separate. No longer was there to be any discrimination based on the color of one's skin. And all the signs were to be removed.

Well, they accomplished the last part. The signs did come down. Now you can move into any neighborhood you want. Your kids can go to the school of your choice with a diverse student body. When you fly on a plane, there is not a "Negro section" in the back of the DC-10.

Of course, that's not the whole story. When's the last time you flew and the plane was filled with African Americans? If you're white, how many blacks live in your neighborhood? How integrated is your child's school? The same old system is essentially still in place: two Americas—one white, the other black.

While living in Washington, D.C., we were all too often surprised by an experience we would have when leaving our Pennsylvania Avenue editing room (just four blocks from the White House). If there was a black individual on the street in front of us trying to hail a cab, and we stood just past him trying to hail one too, the cab driver would ALWAYS pass by the black person and then stop to pick us up. We would insist that the cab take the man he just ignored, and we would wave to that person to come and get into the cab. If we failed to grab the door quickly enough so we could hold it open, the cab would often speed away.

Moving to New York after making *Roger & Me*, we encountered the same phenomenon. So, when we got the green light to do *TV Nation*, we had an outlet to do something about it.

As one of the first segments we shot for the pilot of *TV Nation*, we arranged to have an African American guy stand on a street corner in Manhattan and then, twenty yards down the street from him, a white guy. And just to up the ante, we got Emmy-nominated actor Yaphet Kotto as our black prospect—and Louie Bruno, a convicted felon who served time in four different prisons, as the representative from our race.

So, who would the taxis stop for—a distinguished black actor, or a white criminal? Hmmm.

We set them up on the corner of Amsterdam Avenue and Seventy-sixth Street on New York's Upper West Side. In one of the rare instances on *TV Nation* when we used hidden cameras, we placed one cameraman on the second floor of a building across the street, the other in a parked van.

One by one, the taxis whizzed by Yaphet and picked up Louie. Primetime racism at its best.

Louie Bruno would get into the cab and tell the driver to take him only five blocks. When the taxi stopped, another camera crew

Yaphet Kotto, black guy.

Louie Bruno, white guy.

and our correspondent, Rusty Cundieff, would be waiting to ask the cabbie a few questions.

"Did you see the black guy back there, just before you picked up this guy?"

"Uh, no, I didn't see him," one cabbie replied.

We decided to always take the taxi driver at his word. On the next attempt, we put a huge klieg light on the curb shining right on

---

Catching Racists in the Act

There are many ways you can nab those who discriminate in your hometown, even if they don't hang out a sign or are particular to white sheets. Each of these little experiments requires two of you, one white, one black—and a little time to kill. Here's how:

1: REAL ESTATE AGENTS: Get the Sunday paper's classified section and check out an open house in an all-white neighborhood. Attend separately. Take a little microrecorder and record the comments of the agent as he or she attempts to steer the black customer away from purchasing the house. The next day, call the housing board in your city and play them the tapes. Go to the media. Shut them down.

2: JOG THROUGH A WHITE NEIGHBORHOOD: Again separately, but have a friend videotape this from a car staying a hundred feet back. Eventually, someone will call the cops when they see a black guy running down their street. What else could it be? "HE'S GETTING AWAY WITH SOMETHING!" (Be careful with this one. Unlike the Realtors who come armed only with their bullshit, these cops carry guns and like to pull them on black "suspects.")

3: THE FRIENDLY SKIES: Both of you, white and black, board a plane and plop yourselves down separately in the first-class section. Count the seconds it takes before the flight attendant asks the black passenger, "May I see your ticket" so it can be "verified."

Mr. Kotto. Of course, the next cab passed him by, too, and picked up Mr. Bruno. When Rusty asked that cabbie if he had seen Yaphet, he replied, "Sure, but he looked kinda threatening."

Again, we accepted his answer, and, to make Yaphet look less "threatening," we put a baby in his arms and a bouquet of roses in his hands. The next cabs went right on by.

In fact, it didn't really matter what we did. Yaphet hailed cabs dressed in a tuxedo, as if he were attending the opera or a formal dinner, but it made no difference to the cabbies. We even brought in one of those big portable lighted signs and lettered it with "I Need a Cab," stuck it right next to him, and the taxis would zip on by to collect the white felon.

When Rusty interviewed the drivers, he asked them if they knew whom they had picked up. He showed them a copy of Louie Bruno's arrest record. They were stunned. He gave the cabbies eye tests to see if there might be something wrong with their eyesight that caused them to miss a six-foot four-inch, 250-pound black man. Actually, what they had done was to make a snap decision that Louie looked "safe" because he was *white*.

Finally, Rusty asked the last taxi driver if he discriminated on a regular basis. He said no, he didn't discriminate at all. Rusty said, good, glad to hear that, because I've got a few friends who need a ride uptown. He then motioned over the rap group Run-D.M.C. Louie got out, they got in, and the driver reluctantly headed off to the Bronx.

In fairness to the New York City cabbies, there were a number of them, mostly black, who did pull over to give Yaphet a ride. But they were definitely the minority.

Rusty Cundieff finds out that cabbies can see black on white very clearly.

Raise Your Voice

When you see discrimination taking place, you can take action. Complaints won't eliminate racism, but they do put the cab companies on notice. Whenever you can, make the point of giving your cab to someone on the street that has been "overlooked."

NEW YORK CITY
Taxi & Limousine Commission
Open Monday–Friday,
   9:00 A.M.–5:00 P.M.
212-302-8294 or
   NYC-TAXI
Press "1" at the main
menu to get the complaint
department.

WASHINGTON, D.C.
D.C. Taxicab Commission
202-645-6010
They prefer complaints in
writing, sent to:
D.C. Taxicab Commission
2041 Martin Luther King Jr. Ave.
   SE, Room 201
Washington, D.C. 20020

BOSTON
Boston Police Taxi Department
154 Berkely Street
Boston, MA 02116
617-343-4475

CHICAGO
Dept. of Consumer Services
312-744-9400

SAN FRANCISCO
San Francisco Police Dept.
Taxicab Complaints
415-553-1447

LOS ANGELES
If you see a taxi pass you by in
Los Angeles, check the dosage
of your prescription. You're not
really in L.A.

When the taxi piece aired, it became an instant hit with viewers. Jay Leno called and wanted to do a similar version of it on the street with his band leader, Branford Marsalis. Numerous news shows copied the experiment (without the demented *TV Nation* white-felon twist, of course).

In the end, while we all got a good laugh, it was actually pretty sobering, especially when we learned that our assistant director on the piece (who is black) couldn't get a cab home after the shoot and the white producer of the story, Jim Czarnecki, had to go out on the street and hail one for him.

10

Slaves

Illinois was the first to do it. Michigan and Rhode Island followed the next day. Texas decided to wait five years and Delaware refused to go along with it for over thirty-five years. Kentucky couldn't bring itself to join in for 111 years.

Finally, it was Mississippi that held the distinction of being the last state in the union to outlaw slavery by ratifying the Thirteenth Amendment to the U.S. Constitution. It took *130 years,* until 1995, for Mississippi to approve this simple amendment:

Section 1: Neither slavery nor involuntary servitude, except as a punishment for crime whereof the party shall have been duly convicted, shall exist within the United States, or any place subject to their jurisdiction.

Section 2: Congress shall have power to enforce this article by appropriate legislation.

What was it about these two sentences that so offended the people of Mississippi for well over a century? Did somebody still have a property claim on his family's slaves who had been set free? Were they holding some hope that the good ol' days might come back? Or did the idea of abolishing slavery just seem like one more example of liberals and the big, bad federal government interfering with the states' right to govern themselves?

Whatever the reason, like removing the Confederate flag from the top of state capitols in the South today, the issue of race was a lightning rod and one that most wished to avoid.

But, like the billy club of a Simi Valley policeman, sooner or later it rears its ugly head. In the midst of a spate of black churches being firebombed in 1995, the Black Caucus of the Mississippi State Senate introduced a bill to put Mississippi on the record as abolishing slavery once and for all.

We started thinking. . . . Hey, before they get rid of slavery, maybe *TV Nation* should go down there and get some slaves of our own. The network was always making us cut our budget and, well, what better way to reduce spending than to get people working for no money? (This description is commonly applied to what are called "interns" in the entertainment business and in the White House, but we'll ignore that for now.)

The only thing different about our slaves was that they would be all white and would be owned by our correspondent Rusty Cundieff (who, as luck would have it, is black).

Rusty headed off to Jackson, Mississippi, to take advantage of the American tradition of owning slaves. When he arrived, he bought a classified ad in Jackson's daily newspaper. It read:

SLAVES WANTED
Good, honest work. All races please apply. Room & board provided, plus chance to be on national TV.

Fifty prospective slaves replied. We explained to them that they personally would not be paid, but we would compensate their families so we could own them for a week.

We selected six of the applicants, put them in shackles and irons, and Rusty gave them all new slave names: Billy Bob Cundieff, Newt Bob Cundieff, Bob Bob Cundieff, Jesse Helms Bob Cundieff, Billy Bob Dole Cundieff, and Rush Bob Cundieff.

Rusty takes his slaves for a walk.

The six slaves then set about doing whatever Rusty wanted them to do. They shined his shoes. They brought him mint juleps. They shagged golf balls that he chipped. Rusty carted them around town in the trunk of his car and led them by ropes and chains through downtown Jackson. This provoked an incredible number of curious looks.

The slaves were taken to a country-western bar where Rusty, with his whip cracking, had them all line dance for him. Some patrons of the bar took offense to this, and the white slaves were worried that they would be spotted by people they knew—and get their asses kicked for letting a black guy treat them that way.

Tensions mounted as Rusty hauled his slaves into the Jackson shopping mall. He asked a clerk to hang on to the chain holding his slaves while he tried some pants on. The clerk obliged.

Various Mississippi residents commented that slavery was "probably a good idea for its time" but they no longer thought it was necessary. Most were surprised that their state was the last holdout on abolishing slavery, and none thought that Mississippi should have that distinction.

Rusty took the slaves over to the house of state senator Hillman Frazier, a member of the Black Caucus, to see if he needed any work done. Sure, he said, and while the two of them sat in the shade sipping lemonade, the six slaves mowed the lawn, trimmed the hedges, and took out the garbage. Senator Frazier seemed quite pleased with this.

State senator Hillman Frazier and Rusty enjoy a mint julep and their slaves.

Let it be known that on this day of
_____
in the year of 1995
In The Great State of Mississippi that

Bob Bob Cundieff

is now a free man,
entitled to all the benefits and responsibilities.
_____

Finally, the Mississippi legislature passed the bill and became the last state to ratify the Thirteenth Amendment. It was an emotional moment as Rusty granted each of his Cundieffs their freedom. They all shook his hand, and to the strains of "Born Free," went their happy way down the street in front of the state capitol.

Newt Bob Cundieff even did a somersault as he left. "There goes one happy white boy," Rusty remarked as he bid him a tearful good-bye, the Confederate flag still fluttering on top of the capitol behind him.

Rusty waves good-bye to one happy white boy.

11

A Day with Dr. Death

One night, just after tuning into the CBS *Evening News,* we were surprised when Dan Rather introduced a segment from Pontiac, Michigan. The correspondent began his report this way:

"Dan, we don't want to give the country the impression that everyone in Michigan is killing themselves. . . ."

We knew things in Michigan were bad, but not that bad. What was he talking about?

He was, it turned out, speaking of Michigan's own, Dr. Jack Kevorkian. Dubbed "Dr. Death," Kevorkian had become known for his efforts to help the dying commit suicide. He had invented a contraption that allowed his patients to die a peaceful and painless death. The procedure was usually done in the patient's home, in Kevorkian's van, or a rented hotel room. After the person had passed away, Dr. Jack or his lawyer, Geoffrey Fieger, would tele-

Making beautiful music together.

phone the local authorities to come and pick up the body. That call, in turn, would often lead to Kevorkian's arrest.

Even after four different trials, Kevorkian was undaunted and determined to keep violating laws prohibiting assisted suicide, which he saw as unconstitutional. Each time Kevorkian was hauled into court, he was either acquitted or the case was dismissed. The good doctor keeps on going, continuing his personal mission to assist in ending the lives of those who are enduring incredible pain and suffering.

To date, Dr. Kevorkian estimates he has assisted nearly a hundred suicides.

That's a lot of pretty gruesome work, and we figured it must be mighty depressing. At *TV Nation*, we started wondering—what does Dr. Death do on his day off?

Our segment producer, Paco de Onís, contacted attorney Fieger and suggested that Michael spend a relaxing day with Dr. Kevorkian. No assisted suicides—simply a day off. Fieger was a fan of *Roger & Me* and seemed very open to the idea. He didn't know if the doctor would be interested in our proposal, since he is a very

Dr. Kevorkian gives Mike the push he needs.

serious man. But Fieger was the rock 'n' roll half of the Dynamic Deadly Duo, literally and figuratively (Fieger's brother was the lead singer for The Knack), and he was game.

Within a couple of weeks, Fieger called to confirm that Dr. Kevorkian had agreed to spend the day with Mike. It would prove to be one of the most surreal days we ever spent filming *TV Nation*.

Kevorkian lives alone in a sparse, rented house in suburban Detroit. He is a slight, unassuming man who looks like he'd be happiest doing crossword puzzles and listening to Benny Goodman.

One of the first things he did was to invite Mike to sit down and join him in playing some music. Before you knew it, with Mike at the keyboard and Dr. Jack on his flute, they were making beautiful music together. Bach, Mozart, Chopin—one could only imagine them on tour playing the great halls of the world.

Kevorkian then offered to paint Mike's portrait. The doctor is an accomplished artist. Kevorkian's paintings are stark, often grotesque renderings of his view of the world: severed heads of generals and warmongers, weird images of hell and Nazi Germany, animals preparing for the Apocalypse—think Salvador Dalí on a bad acid day and you pretty much get the picture.

Kevorkian's portrait featured Mike with an apple in his mouth (think Eve in the Garden of Eden).

Next, Mike suggested that the two of them go on a picnic in the park. "We don't even want to mention the word 'death' today," Mike told him. "We want to celebrate life with you. On *our* show, you'll be known not as 'Dr. Death' but as 'Dr. *Life*'!"

At the park, the two of them laid out a blanket and Mike prepared a feast of bologna sandwiches, Doritos, cheese sticks, and other assorted picnic foods. Kevorkian admonished Mike for eating junk food. "That stuff will kill you!" he said.

The list of activities Mike and Jack participated in was enough to bring joy to even the most hardened of career assisted-suicide doctors. They played Frisbee. They flew a kite. They pushed each other on the swing set. (Mike kept his eye on Jack each time Jack gave him an overly enthusiastic push.)

Mike had rented an old convertible, and soon they were off on a Sunday drive to downtown Detroit. The first stop was Henry Ford Hospital, where Dr. Kevorkian did his residency as a young man. In keeping with the theme of celebrating life, Mike took Jack inside to greet the newborns who had just entered this world.

Security soon spotted Dr. Death and stopped us from entering further than the lobby. A hospital administrator came down and told Kevorkian to leave. He was hurt and embarrassed, and Mike felt bad that he had taken him there. We did not expect that kind of reaction from the hospital, and it was certainly no way to treat someone who does not charge a dime in helping those who wish to end their own suffering (as opposed to most hospitals and HMOs, which cause a hell of a lot of the suffering and then have the audacity to charge you for it!).

Mike wanted to cheer Jack up, so he proposed an idea. Just a few blocks down the street from the hospital sat the world headquarters of General Motors. "C'mon, Jack," said Mike, "let's see what's going on."

Mike had not been inside the building since *Roger & Me* was filmed. It was a risky thing to do, but, hey, they were back to celebrating life!

The security guard did a double take when he saw *both* Dr. Kevorkian *and* Michael Moore walking through the front door. The look on his face (and the hand on his gun) said it all: "WHICH ONE DO I TAKE OUT FIRST?"

As they stood in the grand, ornate lobby of GM, Michael asked the good doctor if perhaps he had any, um, "solutions" for the company. At first Kevorkian didn't understand what Mike meant. But then it dawned on him and he smiled.

"Oh, yeah. Maybe."

We headed back to Kevorkian's house for more frolicking, but the weather was getting chilly and we still had the convertible top down. Maybe Dr. K. thought we were trying to send him to an early grave. His mood changed rapidly, and he started to complain about the cold he was getting. When we returned to his place, he told us the day of celebrating life was over and he no longer wanted to participate in our adventure. Attorney Fieger tried to smooth things over so that we could continue shooting, but we didn't want to push the doctor. It had already been a long day.

When we left we hoped that Dr. Kevorkian could be better understood as a man with a cause instead of being the butt of every comedian's joke. He is a man who, whether you agree or disagree with him, has a point. We do a lousy job of caring for our terminally ill citizens. Instead of finding ways to make their last days as comfortable and painless as possible, we've invented the means by which to keep them alive a lot longer while they suffer excruciating pain at an astronomical cost. How humane.

12

Are You Prepared for Prison?

Now that there are over 1.5 million Americans locked up behind bars (that's one out of every eighty adult men), we thought as a public service we should help our viewers prepare for that day when they may join their friends and neighbors in the joint.

We contacted prison advisor Frank Sweeney, who has started helping people who are convicted get ready for that big trip to the Big House.

Frank Sweeney is not just an expert. He's an ex-con who spent twenty-two years behind bars for crimes ranging from mail fraud to assaulting a police officer. Now he's giving advice to recently convicted felons. So get out your pencil and take our "Get Ready for Prison" test. Remember—no cheating. Here's our first question:

Ex-con Frank Sweeney.

QUESTION: In prison, I should work hardest to kiss up to:
A. The guards
B. My cellmate
C. The public defender

ANSWER: B
According to Frank, "You've got to be respectful not only to the staff but to the other convicts. That's even more important than being respectful to the staff. The staff won't kill you, the other men will."

QUESTION: My friends in prison:
A. Choose them
B. Let them choose me

ANSWER: A
Frank feels that "it's best to choose your friends. People that choose you for friends—there might be a reason why they're

choosing you—some kind of a ploy to use you. I'd choose my friends rather than have them choose me."

QUESTION: I've made many friends while in prison. It's a
             good idea to give them my home address.
             True or False?

ANSWER: False
"Your friends that you've made in prison—very bad news. I would never trust anybody that completely. You might later on have some problems with the person you gave your address to and later on he could retaliate against your family."

QUESTION: I'm a finicky eater. Any cuisine tips?

ANSWER: "Since 1973, every federal prison has a Kosher kitchen. What I did, I had a friend of mine in jail who is Jewish and he let me sample his diet and I discovered it was delicious. So, when I got to my initial institution, I made arrangements to see the rabbi. And I persuaded the rabbi that I was Jewish."

QUESTION: What crime is most likely to get me stabbed with
             a homemade knife?
             A. Treason
             B. Mail fraud
             C. Bestiality

ANSWER: C
"I've never heard of anybody in prison for a crime of bestiality. Never, never in my entire prison career. Maybe simply because somebody didn't admit to it, but I've never heard of it."

QUESTION: I'm a man who'd rather not be assaulted by my
             cellmates. True or False?

ANSWER: True

"The possibilities—though the probabilities of being raped are not that great for older men. Generally, homosexual assaults are prevalent in reformatories but not so much in the adult institutions. Simply because of the lack of appeal. When you're thirty-eight and beyond you've long ago lost your boyish charm."

QUESTION: Prison love triangles most clearly resemble:
    A. A hot new French film
    B. The running of the bulls in Pamplona
    C. Ali vs. Frazier in the Thrilla' in Manila
    D. Loving relationships entered consensually

ANSWER: D

"Generally in these homosexual relationships men enter into these relationships consensually. There's very rarely any fighting in the adult institutions over who's who—who's going to dominate who—it's consensual with mutual agreement. I'm not a hetero . . . hetero . . . homosexual, so I never had that—I was never involved in this type of behavior."

QUESTION: The phrase that best describes prison health care is:
    A. Canadian-style single payer
    B. HMO
    C. Not very good

ANSWER: C

"There is no such thing as a health care plan. Prison medical treatment in the facility I was in was not very good. If you have a heart attack, take an aspirin, I'll see you in the morning."

How did you score? If you got more than 70 percent correct, you should do fine during your incarceration.

See you in the showers!

13

I Want to Be an Argentinean

Back in 1982, seven years after the end of the Vietnam war and long before the United States could even think about invading another country, the British were itching to kick some ass. For them, it had been a while since they'd given anyone a good whuppin'. We were actually trying to remember when the time was they didn't need anyone's help to pull themselves out of a jam. Face it, it's been a long time.

But in 1982, Britain was being ruled by the iron hand of Margaret Thatcher. Thatcher came to power in the midst of a massive backlash against the U.K.'s ineffective Labour Party. She and Ronald Reagan became the best of friends as they shared a common political philosophy: defeat communism and make the world safe for corporations.

At the same time, across the world in Argentina, the ruling military junta was not doing well in the eyes of the public. Too many "disappeared" citizens tend to make everybody a little jumpy and upset. What do the leaders of a country do when it looks like they might be removed from power? Start a war!

What better place for the Argentinean generals to invade than a small, insignificant group of islands known as the Falklands, 290 miles southeast of their Atlantic coast. The Argentineans called them the Malvinas, the name the Spanish had given them hundreds of years ago when they "owned" them before the British stole them.

They probably figured the British wouldn't really care if they took them back. One day they sent a bunch of boats out to the islands and set up camp. They informed the Falkland residents that they were now Argentineans.

Thatcher was livid. Even though she (and most Brits) probably needed help locating the Falklands on a map, and even though neither she nor any prime minister had ever visited there, and even though it appeared the main strategic interest in having the Falklands was its sheep, Thatcher declared that the Crown and the Empire had been assaulted and there would be retribution for this attack on the Queen's subjects.

She dispatched an armada of warships and fighter jets to the South Atlantic. Since it would take a few days for them to get there, the British military figured the Argentineans had enough time to get out without a bruise. But the Argentineans weren't that quick.

Within days, the Brits had arrived and, consistent with their history when you put a gun in their hands, they showed no mercy. It only took ten weeks and a thousand dead soldiers, mostly Argentinean, before the Falklands were securely back in the hands of the United Kingdom. The islanders cheered, Thatcher rose to new levels of popularity at home, and Reagan got all hot and happy over how she did it. Within months, he decided to follow.

his heartthrob and invaded the tiny and insignificant island of Grenada.

Eventually the people of Argentina had had enough of the abuse by their own military and rose up against the generals. Soon, democracy won out and Argentina was a new country. Years passed, but the feeling that a group of islands off its own coast was being controlled by another island nation ten thousand miles away still stuck in the craw of many Argentineans.

So, in 1995 the Argentinean government came up with a nonviolent plan to regain control of the Falklands. They made an offer they were sure the islanders wouldn't refuse: If the citizens of the Falklands would vote to become part of Argentina, the government of Argentina would give each and every islander a free gift of $100,000 or up to $800,000 per family, in cash, no strings attached.

It takes a lot of courage to turn down that kind of money. Unless you are a Falklander. The vote never happened. They weren't even interested. Their attitude was, keep your money and don't cry for us. . . .

Imagine if the Argentineans made the same offer to everyone in Newark, New Jersey. Whoa! Where do I sign up! Or what would happen if they visited an economically devastated area of Thatcher's Britain? Would the residents dismiss so quickly the free cash from Buenos Aires? Sure, it's easy for the Falklanders to turn their nose up at the dough—they have received close to $100 million in aid from the U.K. since 1982 for their two thousand residents. But what if the town you lived in was so hard hit that $100,000 per person looked like a pretty good offer—even if it meant renouncing your citizenship?

We decided to test this theory. Our correspondent, Karen Duffy, traveled to Maerdy, Wales, to see if the people there wouldn't mind going Argentinean.

Maerdy, a former mining town, was not in good shape. Over four hundred jobs had been lost, the unemployment rate had more than doubled in the previous five years, and the safety net the Brits had always been so famous for providing was being snipped away.

Karen Duffy leads the Maerdy residents in Spanish lessons.

Its only claim to fame (and the source of a few tourist dollars) was that it is the birthplace of singer Tom Jones.

Karen walked the streets of Maerdy and met the people. From the butcher shop to the pub to the flower stand she posed the question, "If I were to get the Argentinean government to give you $100,000, would you become an Argentinean?"

Needless to say, Karen received an enthusiastic response. It was amazing to see how many people were willing to forgo obedience to the Crown in order to get a few extra pounds to help them make ends meet. It made us wonder how much more loyalty they would have felt if the $1.4 billion that had gone to the Falklands war had gone into saving places like Maerdy.

In order to get everyone in the spirit of becoming Argentinean citizens—and to make it more convincing to the Argentinean government that these people were serious—we held Spanish classes, passed out gaucho hats and scarves, conducted tango lessons in the town square, and got folks to write a letter to the pope encouraging him to make Evita Perón a saint.

We held a big outdoor party and decorated the streets with Argentinean flags, and served Argentinean beef. The whole thing was videotaped by our crew.

With that tape in hand, Karen headed off to London and a scheduled meeting with the Argentinean ambassador. But when Karen got to the point of explaining what she wanted from him— cash in exchange for Argentinean citizenship—the meeting was abruptly halted and she was shown the door. The Argentinean consulate issued a formal protest to the powers that be in the British government who control the BBC (pointing up one of the serious drawbacks of a state-controlled media). This prompted one of the few times *TV Nation* encountered resistance from the executives at the BBC. Word came down to the BBC producers in charge of *TV Nation* that this piece could not air as is.

We did not want to lose this segment. We negotiated with the BBC. Their position was that if we were going to conduct an interview with an Argentinean, it had to be on U.S. soil. So Karen once again attempted an interview with an Argentinean official, this

Karen invites one and all to the outdoor party.

ARGENTINA COMES TO MAERDY

TANGO, GOUCHO MUSIC, FOOD
--a television spectacular--

BBC Television in a co-production with the United States is doing a story about nationalism and identity. We have chosen Maerdy as the location for a television experiment. We will be introducing your community to various aspects of Argentine culture as well as polling people about their feelings regarding England, Argentina, and their sense of identity with the United Kingdom as its sovereign nation. This event is being filmed for a television show called "TV Nation" which takes an offbeat look at many of the issues facing the world today. It will be on the BBC 2 starting in late July and on television in the US.

JOIN US FOR A DAY OF FUN, FOOD, DRINK AND DANCING
Saturday, July 8, 1995
from 2 pm to 6 pm
North Terrace, Maerdy

If it rains, the alternative date for this event is Sunday, July 8, 1995.

time in New York City. He turned out to be less than friendly as well and asked the crew to leave. We had created another international incident.

Undaunted, Karen left the videotape, the letters from the people of Maerdy, and an album of *Tom Jones's Greatest Hits* on the doorstep of the embassy.

As it turned out, the BBC aired "Falklands" as the first segment in their *Best of TV Nation* show.

14

Junk Mail

Do you occasionally find yourself looking forward to opening your mailbox when you get home? What do you hope will be in there? Personal letters from friends and loved ones? Fancy printed checks written to you with big numbers behind the dollar signs? Hell no! No one writes letters anymore, and when was the last time you received the check that's "in the mail"? These days, the computer literate send E-mails, the rest just phone if they've got something to say, and in most cases, they're asking if your check *to them* is on its way.

All that's left stuffed into our mailboxes these days are the bills (which we'd rather avoid anyway) and the junk mail. And there's a ton of that. From the big envelope that screams "YOU HAVE JUST WON $11 MILLION FROM AMERICAN FAMILY PUBLISHERS" to the packet of coupons for Liquid Gold that you'll never use, to the catalogs with models wearing clothes you could never fit into, the old, reliable U.S. mailbox has become nothing but the litter bin of American capitalism. It is the only legal way a company can dump unwanted refuse on your doorstep and get away with it. The fact that they have a quasi-agent of the U.S. government helping them do it is even more appalling. Kind of sad, isn't it? After all, the mailbox is one of the few things that each and every one of us has (assuming you're not one of the two million homeless). Not even the venerable television set (97 percent of all homes have one) can claim that kind of penetration into the population.

One day as we burrowed through the dumpster we used to call our mailbox, we found a letter from one Sgt. Stacey C. Koon, LAPD. It was one of those "direct mail" solicitation letters that are sent out to millions of homes attempting to get you to send some deserving organization a charitable contribution. You know, Save the Children, the St. Vincent DePaul Society, the United Negro College Fund. But this letter was from none of these groups. It was from the L.A. police officer who hit Rodney King in the head. He was asking that we send him a donation of up to $1,000 to help him defray the costs of his legal team as they fought to overturn his conviction. It read, in part:

> . . . *Several years back our precinct had a black, male prostitute in custody. He went into cardiac arrest, but no one would help him because they feared he had AIDS. I gave him mouth-to-mouth resuscitation in an effort to save his life because I felt that was my duty. Unfortunately the man died and yes it turned out he did have AIDS. Does this sound like the actions of a man who is a bigot? Please, please for the sake of justice and for the sake of my wife Mary and our 5 children, help me battle the liberal establishment and see justice done. I have no one else to turn to.*
>
> *Please won't you just send a short note to Mary, encouraging her in this terrible time. Thank you and God Bless you.*

We were amazed. Who did Sergeant Koon think would send a penny to a guy like him? We wanted to know. So we called the company conducting his direct mail appeal and they told us that he had already pocketed thousands of dollars from people who had received the letter. Wow.

Yes, we Americans are a generous people, and the lower our economic class, the more we give. But do we just pony up a few bucks for *anyone* who asks us for a handout? Do we have any standards before we respond with a check to a piece of junk mail?

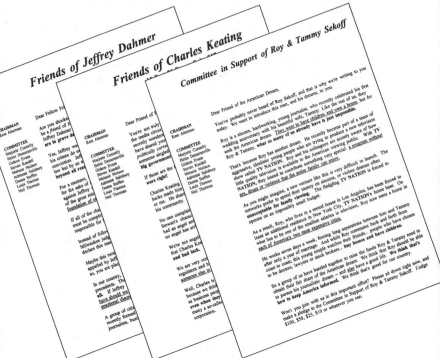

We decided to find out. We contacted David Litwinsky at ALL Direct Mail of New York and asked him to design a number of solicitation campaigns for us. We wanted the whole package—the "personal" letter stating the need for this urgent appeal, the accompanying photos or trinkets that tug at the heartstrings of potential donors, and the envelope that must entice the recipient to open it before chucking it in the trash.

And who would these direct mail appeals be for?

- Charles Keating, the convicted savings-and-loan officer.
- Jeffrey Dahmer, the convicted serial killer and cannibal.
- The Queen of England (enough said).
- Senator Bob Packwood, forced to resign for fondling female staff members.
- Mohammed Salameh, convicted of bombing the World Trade Center.
- And Roy Sekoff, a *TV Nation* correspondent.

The direct mail company had an angle for each of our individuals in need of money. They thought Keating would be the hardest because so many people had their life savings lost through the savings-and-loan scandal. They were sure that most people would not be sympathetic to "a crook." But if we came up with a letter that portrayed Keating as one who believed in our system—make as much money as possible any way you can—then some might see him as a victim. Here is what we wrote:

Fellow American,
. . . Since childhood, all little Charlie Keating wanted to do in life was simply this: to save and loan. If he wasn't talking about saving, he was talking about loaning.

Imagine the great joy then when that ten-year-old boy found out that he wasn't alone, that there were others, thousands of others, just like him, and that there was even a proud name for those people: "savings and loan executives."

. . . If you share these dreams, dreams which Charles Keating is presently in jail for daring to chase, then, fellow American, you're in that jail along with him. Not really, but it's almost as if you are. Either way, you know that appeals are expensive.

"But what about that two billion dollars from his savings and loan?" you may ask. Well, friend, Charles Keating is not on trial here, your future is. And, if you have kids, your kids' future, and if you have kids and your kids have kids then your kids' kids' future. . . .

Dahmer, too, would be difficult. He had, after all, killed and partially eaten a dozen or so young people. But if the letter could focus on his insanity defense, the public would, some of them anyway, understand.

Fellow American,

Let us be blunt. If you think the government is entitled to strictly limit your diet to only fish, fowl, beef, pork, grains, dairy, fruits, vegetables, and legumes, then throw this letter away right now.

But if you think that Man is entitled to sample the culinary pleasures of all God's creatures, including the tender flesh of his fellow Man, please read on . . .

Jeffrey Dahmer is the political scapegoat of vegetarian radicals and self-serving anorexics who know that he is innocent of everything, except for the crime of gastronomical curiosity . . .

As for the charges of cannibalism that have been levied against him, well, all we can say is, they called Hannibal Lecter a cannibal. . . .

The Queen of England—lots of possibilities here. Her castle had burned down, her kids were all nuts, and she was broke. The monarchy was just about over, but most preferred that the Royals go out with some dignity. Major sympathy points.

Dear, Dear American Cousin,

. . . In 1992, as is well known, two of Queen Elizabeth's sons separated from their wives, and her Windsor residence went up in flames.

Her majesty called it her "annus horribilis." Yet even then we, the Friends of the Queen, had scarcely an inkling of the true nature of the horrors which had afflicted her annus . . .

. . . we are counting on you to pay your feudal dues.

Let us not speak of "charity" for it would be unseemly for one of the world's richest monarchs to throw herself at the mercy of poor hardworking common people such as yourselves.

We ask only for what is fair and for what is right: the pecuniary deserts which befit a democratic figurehead whose likeness appears on more than twelve major currencies and the flags of several Third World nations and whose regal doings entertain and engage commoners the world over as they are relayed via the miracle of the modern telegraph to newspapers and wireless. . . .

Former senator Bob Packwood, who was forced to resign in disgrace because of his sexual harassment of the women on his staff, could also be portrayed as a victim who was sorry. Everyone loves to hear those words, "I'm sorry." We are not only a generous people, we are a forgiving lot, too. Our letter for Packwood started this way:

Fellow American,
If you think "fondling" is a four letter word, then throw this letter away right now. But if you think that God meant for men and women to love one another, to support one another, and, yes, to fondle one another, then please read on.
You see, fellow American, I have been accused of fondling women. My name is Senator Bob Packwood.
Maybe I'm out of touch with the new trends and hip styles of these very troubling times . . . But maybe there are some decent Americans still left in this blessed land who are like me—hardworking, patriotic, clean-cut, and yes, inclined to a little fondling when the day is done. . . .

Regarding Mohammed Salameh, the direct mail company felt that our best chances for money would be if we sent the letters to those parts of the country where the people would like to see all of New York blown up.

My dear American friend,
. . . If you think that, in the free expression of one's political opinions, it is unlawful to plant explosive devices in prominent public places then read no further.

But if you have the courage to hear the truth and you care about justice being done, read on.

. . . Sheikh Omar Abdel Rahman has suffered more than words can express in the publicity surrounding the so-called "World Trade Center bombing." . . .

. . . The right to freedom of expression is unequivocally guaranteed under the Constitution and there is no mention of exceptions to the law when it comes to blowing up buildings. . . .

Finally, we thought we'd let the correspondent in this segment, Roy Sekoff, send out his own letter. No reason, really. He just wanted the money. So we said, sure. Let's hit up the American public on behalf of Roy Sekoff.

Dear Friend of the American Dream,

You've probably never heard of Roy Sekoff, and that is why we're writing to you today. We want to introduce this man, and his dreams, to you.

. . . Roy is a sincere, hardworking, young journalist who recently celebrated his first wedding anniversary with his beautiful wife. They want to have children and own a home, but for Roy & Tammy, what so many of us already have is just impossible.

. . . He works seven days a week, forcing long separations between him and Tammy after only a year of marriage. While Roy commutes back and forth from coast to coast, this young couple watches their friends . . . people who have chosen to be doctors, lawyers or stockbrokers . . . buy homes and have children.

We think that Roy should be able to pursue his journalistic dream—and also have a good life. We think that's how to keep America informed. We think that's good for the country. . . .

Marty Gallanter, a direct mail copywriter at ALL Direct Mail, took these concepts of ours, and wrote the letters to send to thousands of preselected addresses around the country.

UNITED STATES
POSTAL SERVICE

November 29, 1994

David Litwinsky
ALL Direct Mail Services Inc
15 E 26th ST FL 9
New York NY 10010

Dear David:

I received and viewed the video you sent me spotlighting TV Nation's segment
on Direct Mail Advertising aired in August.   David, you were terrific in the video!
At the US Postal Service, we are committed to changing the negative perception
which has marked Direct Mail Advertising in the past. And although this
campaign was not aimed at creating a positive perception, it was very effective
in demonstrating the power of Direct Mail Advertising.

Thank You also for sending me copies of the actual letters soliciting pledges. It
is always a pleasure to appreciate the creativity and well honed skills of a good
Direct Mail copywriter. Taken in the context of a fictitious endeavor, they are
nothing short of genius. Congratulations on a great campaign and best wishes in
future projects.

Sincerely,

Deborah J. Maciejewski
Direct Mail Advertising Program Mgr.

A letter of praise, compliments of the U.S. Mail.

After reviewing our budget, we only had the money to send out
three letters, so we narrowed it down to the Friends of Jeffrey Dahmer, the Friends of Charles Keating, and Roy Sekoff. In order to
comply with the law, we had to promise that the actual money we
raised would go directly to the individuals we were soliciting on
behalf of.

So, over twelve thousand letters were mailed, and within three
weeks we started to see the results.

How to Get off Junk Mailing Lists

Want to get rid of that annoying junk mail before it accumulates in your mailbox, or for that matter, your E-mail box?

Call the **Direct Mail Marketing Association** for mail preference service for home addresses only. Dial 202–955–5030 for the pre-recorded Information Hotline for Consumer Services. This is a general mail reduction program; in other words, consumers cannot be removed from specific lists.

Postcards with the consumer's name, home address, and signature should be sent to:
The Direct Marketing Association
Mail Preference Service
P.O. Box 9008
Farmingdale, NY 11735–9008

Requests *must be in writing* for verification purposes (no phone calls), but if people stay on the information hotline, they can order a free pre-addressed postcard. After a processing period of at least 90 days, a gradual reduction in mail will occur.

OTHER HELPFUL RESOURCES
Privacy Rights Clearinghouse
5384 Linda Vista Road #306
San Diego, CA 92110
619–298–3398, phone;
  619–298–5681, fax
www.privacyrights.org
Information on everything from junk mail to caller ID to what to do if your wallet is stolen.

HOW TO GET RID OF JUNK E-MAIL, SPAM, AND TELEMARKETERS
Link to www.ecofuture.org/ecofuture/jnkmail.html for practical tips on how to get rid of junk mail and links to other sites.

Or try www.zerojunkmail.com, a service that for a fee of $25 per year will keep your name off junk E-mail, telemarketing, and E-mail spam lists.

TV Nation Junk Mail correspondent Roy Sekoff
proposes our campaigns to David Litwinsky of ALL Direct Mail.

Yes, folks, we are sad to report that dozens of people sent in their hard-earned money to help these poor souls. Dahmer received the most money. Keating came in second, and Roy came in last. The company broke it down for us this way: had we sent letters to every household in America, our test results indicated that Jeffrey Dahmer would have received $1,205,000, Charles Keating would have received $868,000, and Roy would have got cab fare home.

Why would a serial killer get more donations than a hardworking *TV Nation* correspondent with a beautiful wife and baby?

"It actually has a more rational explanation than you would expect," David Litwinsky told us. "Jeffrey Dahmer is a celebrity. His name draws attention, positive or negative, but celebrity is celebrity, regardless."

"So, you're saying that I would have been better off if I were a convicted felon?" Roy asked.

"You would have been better off as a *famous* convicted felon."

15

Sabotage

The workplace is the only location where someone can yell at you, berate you, force you to do things you don't want you to do, keep you from leaving the premises at the time you planned to leave, make you take drug tests and lie detector tests, withhold payment for services rendered, and generally put you in a position where you feel like you're about an inch tall and all you can do to the boss is smile and say "thank you."

The level of job dissatisfaction and outright anger in the workplace is a subject that is rarely discussed, probably because these days you're lucky to have a job and keep yourself from being downsized, rightsized, or reengineered. The fear of having your hours, pay, and benefits cut back is a full-time emotional preoccupation. Occasionally the frustration will manifest itself in a worker who can no longer take it, snaps, and enters the office with an automatic weapon.

But typically, the abused worker just accepts the situation. Less than 15 percent of the workforce is unionized these days, so most employees lack an advocate defending their rights and have no recourse through which to redress their grievances. In essence they are without a democratic method to be treated with dignity and justice.

But a new phenomenon is sweeping the country. The trend is called Workplace Sabotage—workers getting even by upsetting the way things are "supposed to be." The forms of sabotage include everything from lifting a legal pad out of the office supply cupboard to wiping out tons of critical information on the company computer system. All of it is illegal, and all of it is happening more and more often.

Martin Sprouse compiled the stories of 135 workers who had committed various forms of sabotage and published them in a book entitled *Sabotage in the American Workplace: Anecdotes of Dissatisfaction, Mischief and Revenge.* One of our segment producers, David Van Taylor, suggested we use Sprouse's book to explore the world of sabotage and convince a number of the saboteurs to appear on camera and tell us how they get away with it. Ben Hamper, a former assembly-line rivethead, was the correspondent.

Flint native Ben Hamper reports on Sabotage.

The stories of sabotage that were told or demonstrated to us seemed to have one theme: The worker, powerless, finds a creative way to exact his or her revenge/justice.

Take Harvey (no real names are used). He works as a muralist at one of the Disney theme parks. Like others who work there, he calls the place "Mouseschwitz" because the rules employees must follow seem as if they were written by the SS. For example, no one is allowed to question Disney policy, everything must be done exactly by the book, and dissension is not tolerated. The rigid control the bosses exert over the workers has long been a source of unpleasantness, and a few years ago the workers who play Disney characters like Mickey Mouse formed a union.

Harvey, who does not belong to a union, told us about a manager who was standing over his shoulder telling him how to do his mural painting—"That color is wrong, it's not happy, that man's face doesn't look happy, those flowers should be brighter, happier. Everybody has to be happy." Happy. Happy! HAPPY!

So what did Harvey do to make sure his boss was happy?

Author Martin Sprouse.

In a mural featuring a huge Disney hotel, he painted a Nazi guard surveying the crowd from the balcony. His boss noticed this and asked him, "Who's that guy on the ledge, he looks like a soldier." Harvey explained, "Oh, no, that's actually a security guard. It's good to show security guards, it gives people a safe secure feeling and lets those with crime on their minds know that they had better think twice."

The boss liked that. So he let him leave the "security guard" in the mural—even though the guard had grenades hanging off his belt, a bayonet on his gun, and a strange little mustache.

To this day, the Nazi is still in the mural, though Harvey prefers not to disclose the exact location because he would like it to remain there.

Although Harvey's sabotage will endure for years, some workers are far more impulsive and much more direct in their revenge. Sean's job did not involve any of his artistic skills. Sean worked as a parking valet at one of those swank hotels off Sunset Boulevard in Beverly Hills. His boss, the general manager of the hotel, would fly off the handle without provocation, fire people at will, then take a six-week vacation. This behavior really got on Sean's nerves.

One morning the general manager pulled into the hotel at 6:30 A.M. Sean was the only valet on duty. The doorman wasn't there yet. Sean saw this moment as his opportunity to get even. He got in the boss's Mercedes, drove it down into the parking garage, and then backed it up as fast as he could into a parking space, smashing it into the wall. Then he put it in forward, pulled up, then into reverse, and BAM!, smashed it again. Back and forth he repeated this action until the $50,000 car was wrecked just enough—but not totaled (which would have given the boss a new car).

Sean then walked upstairs, told the manager he had a little trouble parking the vehicle, and quit.

Other workers told us that they have participated in actions that are considered sabotage but can't get them arrested. Work slowdowns are typical. If everyone participates, it is very difficult for the boss to fire everyone, and sooner or later he will have to address the grievances.

Sometimes, the sabotage takes on a political nature. Reggie got a job at the Heritage Foundation in Washington, D.C. The Heritage Foundation is a leading right-wing think tank and was responsible for many of the policies adopted by the Reagan and Bush administrations. If there is a seat of evil in our nation's capital, it is the Heritage Foundation.

Reggie started reading some of the foundation's literature and was appalled by their attitudes toward the poor, women, and working stiffs like himself. His boss liked to brag that he was to the right of Genghis Khan. Reggie needed the job, but he couldn't square the work he was doing with his conscience.

So he had an idea. It was his job to open the mail and forward all the donations to the treasurer's office. Instead, he would take the contributions and simply run them through the shredder. Thousands of dollars ended up being nothing more than confetti in the trash. Reggie noted that the Heritage Foundation was heavily dependent on its fund-raising, and the loss of a few thousands dollars could really put a dent in the organization. Reggie never got caught and eventually found a new job.

The network really, really hated this piece. No matter how many disclaimers we put on it saying how wrong it is to break the law, the suits knew we had hidden sympathies with these saboteurs. We did understand why they did what they did, even though we believed it was actually better to organize unions on the job, sue employers who break the law, and work for legislation that protects workers' safety and rights.

But that all seems overwhelming when you are the one pushing the broom and feeling entirely powerless in a society that rewards greed in the corporate suites but believes you should pay for your own health care from your $6.00-an-hour paycheck.

The network, being an employer, did not want to encourage workplace sabotage. It felt that putting us on the air was sabotage enough.

16

Yuri, Our
TV Nation Spy

The issue of downsizing and the unemployed has been a paramount concern of ours for some time. So it seemed natural to us to help out one of the most detested groups of unemployed people in the world: the former agents of the KGB.

For the nearly fifty years of the Cold War, the KGB acted as the premier spy agency of the old Soviet Union. They were considered to be the most ruthless of espionage agents. They stole atomic secrets from the United States and made their own atomic bomb. They took advantage of our "open" system to gather all kinds of information that was impossible for the U.S. to discover in the Soviet Union. They created such a massive ring of informants around the world that they were able to scare the bejesus out of everyone except James Bond.

Then, one day, it was all over. No more USSR, no more KGB.

What happened to all those spies when they had to come in from the cold? How were they surviving without a weekly paycheck? Who would hire such a sneaky bunch of amoral, conniving bastards?

We would!

We thought it would be cool to have our own secret agent working for the show. We would become the first network program with its own KGB agent who would be on assignment to do, well, uh, whatever we wanted him to do.

We placed an ad in a Russian-language newspaper in New York, figuring that a number of these spies who had been assigned to the U.S. must have been stuck here when the Soviet Union fell apart. The ad said that we were looking for "former KGB agents" to work for us on a primetime TV show. No questions asked.

KGB - National network television show seeks to hire former KGB Agent to be an on-air reporter. This unusual opportunity does NOT involve discussing any aspect of your previous career. Call ROGER at

We received dozens of replies. It was a remarkable indication of just how many commies there are among us. A lot who responded weren't actual agents but "informants." They didn't count. We wanted the real deal, the professional spy who could kill for us in a blink of an eye, if that's what we wanted.

Eventually, we called about six KGB pros into our office for an official interview. It was not the typical "meet the boss" session:

Q: How many people have you killed?

A: More than you need to know.

Q: Show us your most lethal move.

A: On you, or your intern?

Q: Have you ever met Rupert Murdoch?

A: This is still classified information.

The agents told us incredible stories of derring-do and narrow escapes. In a way, we could sense that they missed the old days when they would sneak through the Berlin Wall or stow away on a freighter to Liverpool to participate in a major undercover operation. They were trained for one thing and one thing only. Now what were they to do? Wait tables? Pump gas? Become sports agents?

We respected their skills and thought they could come in handy on a show that was constantly battling with network superiors (Capitalist Swine!). Our survival depended on the programming the competition on the other networks was offering (Our Mortal Enemies!). We needed something to create a balance of power—our own sort of nuclear deterrent, if you will.

And we found it in Yuri Shvets.

Yuri was a ten-year veteran of the KGB. He had infiltrated the U.S. by posing as a correspondent. He applied for and received press credentials on Capitol Hill, giving him easy access to our legislative bodies while all the time collecting

Yuri Shvets, TV Nation's KGB spy.

data on what our congressmen were up to. (Actually, he could have saved himself a lot of work by simply watching C-SPAN.)

Yuri had multiple skills, spoke good English, and had a suave way that we knew would disarm anyone who met him. To test his loyalty to us, we asked him if he would do anything for us. "Yes, anything," he replied.

Then go jump out of a plane!

The next day, he did just that. On our orders, he thrust himself out the door of a single-engine plane flying at ten thousand feet. No questions asked.

Yuri was our man.

We came up with a number of missions we wanted him to consider. They included:

1. Find out why the cost of undercoating is never included in the price of a new car.

2. Find out who those "John 3:16" guys are and remove them from all ball games.
3. Track down Yakoff Smirnoff and eliminate him.
4. Find out who "Jeff Craig of *60 Second Previews*" is and why he's always quoted in every movie ad.
5. Find out what the black box from an airplane is made out of and get us some of that material.

Yuri was game for anything. In the end we came up with three separate missions that we felt would have the most impact on the survival of the planet.

Mission #1: Find Out Who Is Actually Buried in Nixon's Grave

None of us really believe that Richard Nixon is dead. He was so tricky during his lifetime that there *is* the possibility he's tricked us once again and is actually alive somewhere.

Just the thought of that was too much for us to handle.

Yuri, too, was eager to find out the truth, as Nixon was once his adversary. He accepted our mission with enthusiasm.

Yuri started his investigation in the last place Nixon was seen alive—New York Hospital. Nixon went there the night before his death and was released with a clean bill of health. The next night, he was back. Although many hospital personnel saw Nixon alive when he was admitted, Yuri could find no one who would say they saw his dead body being wheeled out. No one.

Yuri went out to Park Ridge, New Jersey, where Nixon had been living in recent years. He asked the neighbors what they knew. "One day he looked fine, the next day he was gone!" one stunned neighbor told Yuri. Nixon was seen out walking his dog just a few days before his "death." No sign of a man about to die.

Yuri then stopped by the place where Nixon is known to have had his last meal, an Italian restaurant in Edgewood. The owner said Nixon downed a healthy order of pasta and looked completely well.

It appeared that even some of Nixon's closest friends were perplexed as to the cause of Nixon's death.

Nixon's best friend, Robert Abplanalp, couldn't understand how it happened. "The night the President died, I left the hospital two hours before, thinking, gee, he looks *great*," Abplanalp told the *New York Post*.

Yuri agreed. He spoke with the ambulance people and the hearse driver and the military escort that took his "body" to its final resting place at the Nixon Library in California. Not one of them could say if they actually saw Nixon's remains being placed in the casket.

"It was a closed-casket funeral," remarked one military guard. "Kind of strange to have a closed casket when the guy hasn't been in a big car wreck or something."

Yuri finally headed out to Nixon's grave in Yorba Linda, California, to discover once and for all if Nixon was actually buried there. The security force at the grave site was very intense and would not allow Yuri to exhume the body, even though he had gone to all the trouble and expense of bringing his own shovel.

Yuri on assignment in Southern California.

The truth that Nixon might still be alive sets in.

He did pluck a few blades of grass from atop the grave and reported that this did not feel like grass growing in soil with human remains buried in it.

Although he could not bring us conclusive proof, he did have this to offer:

"Look at who's running for president this year [1996]. Bob Dole ran the Republican National Committee for Nixon. Pat Buchanan was Nixon's speechwriter. Pete Wilson was an advance man for the Nixon gubernatorial race in 1962. Even if Nixon's body may be gone, his spirit lives on in many ways, inside many men wearing bad suits and a five o'clock shadow."

Mission #2: Find the Heart and Soul of the Democratic Party

This assignment was a little more difficult. Yuri was assigned to find out why the Democrats try so hard to sound like Republicans and why they have forgotten they are the party of working people.

Where had the soul of the Democrats gone? Why was it full of wimps and people of little or no conviction?

Yuri found the answers at a semi-annual meeting of the Democratic National Committee in New Orleans. There, he listened to speech after speech denouncing welfare recipients, calling for adjustments in Social Security and Medicaid, and supporting the elimination of affirmative action. Hey, Yuri thought, there's already a party that believes in those things—it's called the *Republican* Party.

Only former Clinton campaign manager James Carville provided a counterpoint to all this quasi-Republicanism. He told the gathered that they must stick to their guns, have the courage of their convictions, and not lose sight of the traditional platform of the Democratic Party.

Few seemed interested in his advice.

Yuri concluded that if the Democrats were to remain a true party, they should stand for something. That, it seemed, was a long way off and there was nothing Yuri could do to save them.

Mission #3: Find Out What Our Competition Is Up To and Destabilize Them

The year we were on Fox, we were scheduled in the thrilling time slot of 8:00 P.M., Friday nights. What are YOU doing at eight o'clock on a Friday night? NOT WATCHING TV, RIGHT?!

We were up against *Diagnosis: Murder* on CBS, *Family Matters* on ABC, and *Unsolved Mysteries* on NBC. We told Yuri to go and gather information on the competition and do whatever damage he saw fit.

He reported back that he had never seen anything like the security he encountered at *Diagnosis: Murder* and *Family Matters*. It was "tighter than the Kremlin" and he was frustrated that he was unable to penetrate it.

But at *Unsolved Mysteries*, hosted by actor Robert Stack, Yuri was welcomed onto the set, where he talked to everyone from the producer to the hairstylist. The secret he learned? You have to look

Mike's makeover.

really, really good if you are going to have a successful TV series. He was amazed at the transformation they gave the seventy-year-old Robert Stack.

"You need to get this makeup artist for Michael," he wrote in his communiqué. "And for God's sake, get him a new wardrobe."

We complied. At the end of the show that week, Mike came out dressed in Armani, wearing contact lenses, and his hair had been combed. He looked like a half a million bucks.

The results? *Unsolved Mysteries* beat us again in the ratings that week.

When the producers of that show found out we had sent a KGB agent onto their set, they called their lawyer and threatened to sue. We threatened to send Yuri back—and this time, he wouldn't be full of glasnost.

They backed off. The next time we saw the *Unsolved Mysteries* producers was at the Emmy Awards, when we were up against each other in the same category. We won. Yuri had nothing to do with it.

Honest.

17

Mike's Missile

If it seems we spent a lot of time on *TV Nation* coming to terms with the end of the Cold War, it's probably because we, like everyone else born between 1947 and 1989, knew there was a very real possibility that the world could end at any minute. For most of our adult lives we lived with the threat of the "Evil Empire" of the Soviet Union. The godless, robotlike communists who were slaves to the state were so powerful, so scary, that we believed they could end the world at any minute just because, well because they felt like it.

This fear successfully became the cornerstone of U.S. foreign policy, created deep rifts at home, caused the deaths of millions of Asians and tens of thousands of Americans in two Asian wars, and nearly did blow up the world during the Cuban missile crisis.

But in 1989–1990, the Cold War was over in the blink of an eye, thanks to the guy with the spot on his head. We weren't quite sure what happened. One day Mikhail Gorbachev decided the arms race was finished and unilaterally quit (the USA kept building the bombs). The next day, when he decided that democracy was a good thing, the Berlin Wall was dismantled, and people all over the Soviet Union and Eastern Europe celebrated free elections, freedom of religion, and the right to become capitalists and watch the old Soviet neighborhood swirl right down the drain. And with it went the possibility we would get to see nuclear Armageddon.

Well, not exactly.

You see, the forty thousand nuclear weapons each side built during those forty-two years are still active, alive, and ready to be launched. Why has it not been the number one priority of the Clinton administration to eliminate these missiles worldwide? What is the need for them? To protect us from Grenada? Panama? Iraq? Please.

It is true that both sides started to dismantle some of the bombs, but then came the news that there are missing containers of plutonium. Other countries were buying up nuclear technology on the black market. (India? Pakistan?) The instability of the former territories of the Soviet Union makes us wonder who has his finger on "the button" at this very second.

With a sense of trepidation and a healthy dose of American superiority, we decided to travel to Russia to see if we could find the missile that the Soviets had targeted at Flint, Michigan, during the Cold War. Where was this missile today? Who was in charge of it? Was it still unnecessarily being pointed at us? Did somebody run off with it? Could we buy it? Could we just have it, please?

Every major city, industrial area, and military base in the United States and the USSR was targeted by the other side for total destruction. Because Flint had the largest concentration of General Motors factories in the country (all of which were used to build weapons during World War II), we figured our city was definitely on the short list for the dustbin. We imagined a special nuclear device aimed right at us, ready to be launched at a moment's notice. A flick of the switch, and bye-bye hometown.

We were able to obtain declassified Pentagon documents verifying our hunch. The papers showed that not only was Flint expected to be wiped off the map, the Defense Department had even pinpointed the

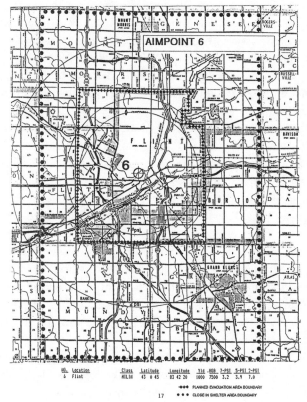

NO.	Location	Class	Latitude	Longitude	Yld	HOB	7-PSI	5-PSI	2-PSI
6	Flint	MILIN	43 0 45	83 42 20	1000	7500	3.2	3.9	7.0

♦♦♦ PLANNED EVACUATION AREA BOUNDARY
● ● ● CLOSE-IN SHELTER AREA BOUNDARY

17

Ground zero in Flint.

exact spot where they believed the Russians would drop the bomb. It
stated that the corner of Bluff and Cadillac streets in Flint was the pro-
jected ground zero, right in front of a GM engine plant.

These facts were confirmed by John West, the Civil Defense
director for the Flint area. As we stood there on that corner with him,
we wondered why on earth the Russians would still want to level a
part of America that had already been leveled by General Motors.
Plus, it was on that street corner that the workers of Flint began the
country's union revolution in 1936. Why would our comrades want
to eradicate such an important piece of proletarian history?

It made no sense to us. We decided to try to buy the missile. So we asked the network, NBC, to give us $10,000 in cash so that we could go to Russia and liberate "our" missile. They consented. (You're probably wondering, what line item did this fall under at NBC? "Let's see, we've got Seinfeld's salary, Jay Leno's new set design—oh, yeah, and Mike Moore wants to pick up a nuclear warhead on his trip to Moscow.")

We also researched and obtained more declassified documents showing how to dismantle a Soviet missile. We decided to bring along a "Map of the Stars' Homes" from Beverly Hills, California. We figured, if they wouldn't sell us the missile, maybe we could try to take it apart or, at the very least, convince the Russians to redirect it away from Flint—say, toward Brentwood, California.

When we arrived in Moscow with our briefcase full of cash and declassified documents, we began a series of "incentives" to get our loot and missile dismantling plans into the country. In the new Russia, the dollar is king, and by flashing a few of them in front of anyone who stands in your way, you can go just about anywhere you want.

We had arranged a series of meetings with the ambassadors from the Ukraine and Kazakhstan to make sure they did not possess the Flint missile. They assured us that they only had weapons pointed at Western Europe and China and, besides, they had no clue how to launch them. The Russians took the launch codes with them when they left.

We met secretly with former KGB agents and members of the opposition parties, but none of them could help us locate the missile aimed at Flint.

We learned that the new president, Boris Yeltsin, would be speaking in Red Square, so we showed up to see if he could help us. During the speech, Mike climbed up on the flatbed truck that served as a stage and tried to get close to him. Unable to get him to stop speaking and give us the directions to the Flint missile, Mike, in one of the weirdest moments ever on *TV Nation,* turned to the

audience and, standing right beside Yeltsin, began making his own speech to the people.

"Citizens of Russia—I come in peace. I also come to buy the missile you had pointed at me. I bring American currency. Will you help me? No Nukeski Flintski!"

Although thousands were present, no one seemed to have any idea where Mike's missile was.

We were beginning to give up hope when we learned of a former Soviet colonel who had run a missile base and was willing to talk to us. He agreed to meet Mike, but he had an unusual request: he asked Mike if he would do the interview in the nude, at a Russian bath.

So, in the midst of dozens of naked Russian men (all of whom were digitally castrated before the show could air), the colonel told Mike that he had run a missile base north of Moscow and that the missiles there had been pointed at the "middle western" part of the United States. He did not know the specific cities, although Detroit sounded familiar.

That was good enough for us, so off we went to Zvneyord Missile Base. In a nearby village we stopped at a house to ask for directions and were invited in for vodka and fried eggs. The Russians sang a love song to Kathleen, and everyone had more vodka. Just the shape to be in when you're getting ready to take a nuclear device apart.

We headed out on a highway and soon turned down the country road that would lead us to the base. As we approached our destination, we saw the universal sign for DO NOT ENTER all around warning us to immediately turn away. We decided to press ahead until we came to a large metal gate. Posted there was a typical *American* STOP sign—in English.

There were no guards to be seen, so Mike got out and knocked on the gate. No one answered. He then tried climbing the wall. At that moment two soldiers approached, ordered him away from the wall, and told the van driver to put the vehicle in reverse—or else.

We hightailed it out of there and down the drive. We were definitely trespassing at this point, and to make matters worse, we noticed a fire truck approaching our van at a high speed. Although

Our international crew for the Missile shoot.

we were in the middle of nowhere, we assumed that there must be a fire someplace nearby. As the truck got closer and started crossing the center line toward our van, we saw that soldiers were hanging off it, with guns pointed at us, motioning for us to pull over. (We learned later that because the country was in such shambles, there were few replacement parts for army vehicles, so as trucks and tanks broke down, the Soviet army commandeered whatever vehicle they could. They were now down to using fire trucks to protect an intercontinental ballistic missile base. Some superpower.)

We slowed down to assess our situation. They ordered our van to stop and told the driver to get out. Our Russian interpreter was scared and told us it would be best to turn the camera off. But our cameraman, Alexander Zakrewski, a Pole, kept rolling and said, "Zees is not a problem," in his heavy accent. We all tried to reminisce about the last time we had a rifle pointed at us, and damned if this wasn't the first time!

For nearly two hours we negotiated with the soldiers. They took our passports, our photos, and our "papers." Luckily, we had "papers" with us—props we had assembled. The soldiers were impressed, though. Like a scene from an old war movie, they meticulously examined each document. They demanded the videotapes we had just shot at the gate and told us they were taking us in. Alexander kept rolling tape and Michael started telling jokes in the van to help break the tension. Our driver then did something that saved all of us. He convinced the soldiers that if they took our tapes, and the authorities found that we had done nothing wrong, they would be responsible for reimbursing us for those tapes. This sent an unexpected wave of fear through the ranks. They were already living in poverty and paid so poorly that to pay us for our tapes could cost them all a week's salary. So they backed off and, in a compromise, scribbled out a confession for us all to sign and then we could go.

We thanked them for their kindness, Kathleen took Polaroids of all of us with all of them to give to their kids, and we got the hell

*Our "papers" came in handy
at Zvneyord Missile Base outside Moscow.*

out of there. Somewhere, in the middle of all of this, the vodka had
begun wearing off.

We had risked our lives, yet still no missile. Back in Moscow, our
last appointment was with an elderly man, Sergei Sergovich, whose
old job in the Kremlin had been managing all the missile sites. We
met him, his wife, and his grandson in their small, homey apartment in the outskirts of the city.

Michael immediately asked him how to get to the Flint missile.
Sergei said that he could tell us but that it was a great secret. He
asked Michael, "Why are you worried so much? Who is scaring you
and telling stories about us?" Sergei explained to us that he always
thought the Cold War was a stupid idea and that no one in Russia
wanted to see the world come to an end. They just thought that's
what we all wanted.

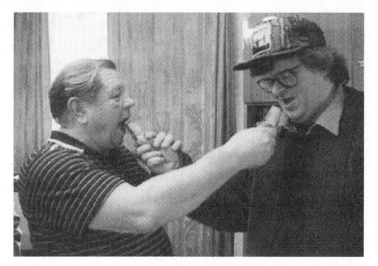

Comrades join in a Twinkie toast.

Not true, we told him, none of us wanted that either. So what was all the commotion about? Only fear had kept us apart. We finally all just laughed, sang songs, and traded gifts. Sergei gave us—what else?—more vodka, and we gave him a box of Twinkies. Then we toasted, Michael and Sergei entwining arms and each biting off a hunk of a Twinkie.

Old enemies were now good friends.

18

Haulin' Communism

Sure, we had fun with the end of the Red Menace. We assisted the Pentagon in finding a new enemy. We gave work to an unemployed Soviet spy. Yet, overall, there was something sad about it all.

It caught all of us by surprise. When The Who broke up, they went on one last farewell tour to give their fans a chance to say good-bye. Great athletes have done the same. Who can forget the final year Nolan Ryan pitched his last games in each city and fans packed the stadiums? Remember Kareem's last season in the NBA? Everyone wanted to see him play one last time and wish him well.

But the Soviet Union, and its unique brand of communism, just disappeared without so much as a "see ya" to the rest of us.

Communism deserved a final tour. The crew at *TV Nation* was determined to make that happen.

So, we rented a huge 18-wheeler truck and ordered it painted bright red with a huge golden hammer and sickle on each side. We then loaded the truck with ten thousand pieces of communist paraphernalia: hundreds of Little Red Books, copies of *The People's Daily*, tapes of "The Internationale," old Soviet uniforms, a painting of Karl Marx, and flags from the USSR, East Germany, Poland, and North Korea.

We even invited Gus Hall, four-time presidential candidate from the Communist Party USA, to climb aboard.

We hired Al Wallach, a trucker from Brooklyn, to drive this vehicle across the country, and on a Friday morning in New York's Union Square we christened our big red communist truck and wished Al well as he headed off across America for "Communism's

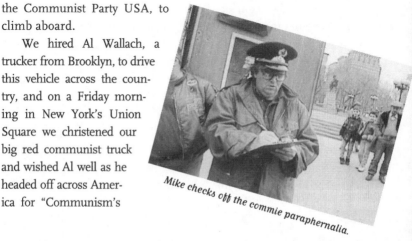

Mike checks off the commie paraphernalia.

Last Ride." His mission was to stop in towns and villages, at church socials and PTA functions, to give the American people a chance to bid a fond and tearful farewell to an ideology that, at least on paper, seemed like a wonderful concept:

> *From each according to his ability,*
> *to each according to his needs.*

In case Al was stopped by the police for any innocent infraction of the law, he carried with him this statement:

I AM NOT NOR HAVE I EVER BEEN A COMMUNIST. I AM A TRUCKER HIRED BY A COMPANY NAMED SPECTRE TO HAUL COMMUNISM ACROSS THE COUNTRY. I DRIVE IN PEACE AND DO NOT ADVO-CATE THE VIOLENT OVERTHROW OF THE AMERI-CAN GOVERNMENT. I AM JUST A WORKING MAN HAULING LITERATURE ADVOCATING THE VIOLENT OVERTHROW OF THE AMERICAN GOVERNMENT. GOD BLESS AMERICA.

While driving down the New Jersey Turnpike, Al needed a bathroom break. As the truck sat in the parking lot of Big Boy underneath the Exxon sign, curious travelers came over to check it out. A man wanted to know if Ho Chi Minh was inside. A couple of guys started dancing like Russian Cossacks. It seemed as if our trip was going to go quite smoothly, bringing a bit of joy to those we encountered. (Of course, we were in New Jersey, so just about any-thing would bring joy to those people's lives.)

Leaving the Garden State, we entered Pennsylvania and the city of Philadelphia, the birthplace of our Liberty. We thought it would be cool if Al drove the truck up to the Liberty Bell and rang it once. The National Park Police did not like that idea—in fact, no one can ring the Liberty Bell anymore because its crack might just go all the way through—and then, well, no more Liberty.

Al respected how fragile our Liberty actually was, so he drove south to our nation's capital, Washington, D.C., in the hopes of getting the President to come out and greet the truck on its last tour.

The big red communist truck with its hammer and sickle slowly crept along Pennsylvania Avenue, the Main Street of our democracy. Al pulled the 18-wheeler right up along the curb in front of the White House and hopped out. He was immediately surrounded by a phalanx of Secret Service agents who demanded to know what the hell he was doing.

"I'm just haulin' some communism, sir," Al replied nervously, fingering the statement he kept in his pocket.

"There's no truck allowed to park here, communism or no communism," came the stern reply from one of the agents. "Move this thing outta here or we're giving you a ticket."

That's all it really took to rid the truck and its communist ideology from Washington, D.C. The *threat* of a *parking summons!* Why didn't we think of that during the Cold War? Imagine the billions of dollars we could have saved on the arms race.

Al jumped back in the truck and pulled away. Oddly, the next month, barricades were erected to divert traffic away from Pennsylvania Avenue in front of the White House. We like to think it had something to do with our big red communist truck, but, in fact, it had more to do with the five assaults on the White House from crazy citizens (including a dive-bombing pilot) with easily obtained weapons.

The most treacherous portion of the trip now confronted Al: the Deep South. Not exactly a hotbed of socialist activity. As he cruised down the highway, other truckers were giving him dirty looks, and soon CB radios were burning up with the news of a "big commie truck" spotted on the interstate. Various truckers plotted ways to "deal with" the truck, and one CBer hoped that our commie cargo included Hillary Clinton. All of this chatter made Al even more nervous.

In southern Virginia, Al drove to Jerry Falwell's church in Lynchburg. He drove round and round the church hoping to smoke Falwell out, but Falwell stayed inside and never did say "good-bye."

At local truck stops, Al became both a mini-celebrity and a target. More than one trucker came up to him and asked. "Whatcha got in there?" and Al would reply, "Just a bunch of communism."

At one watering hole, Al opened up the back of the truck and brought some of the literature inside to read. He had started wondering what this commie political system was all about. There he sat with his burger and fries, poring over Mao's Little Red Book and *The Communist Manifesto*. A guy at the next table was infuriated, and he told Al that he'd rather haul the worst toxic waste than that Bolshevik crap.

"Ain't ever haulin' any communist shit," the trucker muttered. Al put away his Little Red Book.

The tension mounted as Al headed through the Carolinas, Georgia, and Alabama. Cops trailed the truck. Guys in pickups flipped the bird. Even though communism was no longer a threat, just the sight of the truck was too much for some to handle.

And so it was, after the truck was parked just outside the Best Western in Demopolis, Alabama, that someone chose to firebomb it.

Al had just walked over to a nearby convenience store to buy some snacks, and when he returned the truck cab was on fire and the fire department was pulling in to put out the blaze. The police investigated and ruled it a probable arson, but did not apprehend the culprit.

It was a setback, but we ordered a new cab for Al, and within a day he was off to finish communism's "March to the Sea." Actually, we ran out of capitalist cash—we had only enough money to send Al to New Orleans instead of all the way across the country. And, there was another problem. We had discovered in our research that transporting communist paraphernalia is still illegal in Louisiana under the Criminal Code, Section 14.358, titled "The Subversive Activities and Communist Control Law." In the interest of full disclosure we had faxed Al a copy of the Louisiana declaration of public policy, and he wisely decided to look it over. Al read, " 'Words are bullets' and the communists know it and use them so." It went on: ". . . this state is a stopping place or 'way station' for sizeable shipments of dangerous communist propaganda to the rest of the United States and to many foreign countries." Furthermore, Al read that any person who violated these provisions could be fined up to

Firefighters respond to the call.

There's Still Time to Be a Commie

If you were born just a little too late to get in on the Red Menace, not to worry—they're still with us!

The Communist Party USA is not only alive and well, it is also a with-it organization. Refusing to be left behind in the computer age, they have their own Web site and Internet activities. They publish a very good newspaper, the *People's Weekly World*; a journal, *Political Affairs*; and still sell the old stand-bys like Marx and Engels's *The Communist Manifesto*.

Check 'em out. Maybe next time they won't find themselves supporting regimes that like to keep a lid on their own people.

800 number
1-800-923-8061 (if the FBI cuts you off, call back at 1-212-989-4994)

Web site
www.hartford-hwp.com/cp-usa

E-mail
cpusa@rednet.org

People's Weekly World E-mail
pww@pww.org

Cuban Interests Section
1-202-797-8518

$10,000 or imprisoned at hard labor for up to six years, or both.

Because Al is a law-abiding citizen, and because he had already crossed the state line and traveled into Louisiana, and because he wanted to serve as little time as possible in a Louisiana jail, he decided the best thing to do was to go to the nearest state police post and turn in himself, the truck, and all the commie junk.

The desk sergeant was confused. Al showed him a photocopy of the Louisiana statute:

> It is the duty of the sheriffs of the respective parishes, upon the finding of any bulk storage of any communist propaganda, to enter upon the premises where the material is found, clear the premises of all human occupants, and padlock the premises until judicially ordered to reopen them.

The desk sergeant looked at the document, looked at the big red commie truck, and looked at Al. "Bottom line, I'm not worried about it and you shouldn't be either," he said.

Al finally made it to the Gulf of Mexico, where the ten thousand pieces of communist propaganda were loaded onto a barge and sent off to sea. He stood on the shore and waved a fond farewell. He had grown close to the ideology on the trip, and it was sad for him to see it disappear into the sunset.

As you can imagine, this was not one of the easiest segments to get on the air. When the executives saw the lengthy eighteen-minute cut, they were convinced we were promoting socialism. When we realized they were onto us, we cut the piece back to nine minutes, including dropping the "barge" section, and got it past the censors. It became one of the most popular segments in the *TV Nation* series. It will certainly go down in the history books as the only time Gus Hall appeared in a primetime entertainment show seen by more people than had voted for him in his four previous presidential elections.

Sometimes, there is justice.

19

The Johns of Justice

You know the scene. You are at a concert or a movie or a ball game and the guys who "have to go" run in and out of the men's room in record time—no waiting, no hassles, no need to clean up after themselves.

But over at the entrance to the ladies' room, it's another story. The line stretches out the door and down the hall. Ever so slowly it inches forward, as if women's kidneys were built of a material far different and stronger than men's. What is worse? The struggle to hold "it" or the hold that seems to be on The Struggle? Feminism is so passé these days. Oh, look—only another thirty-two women before you can relieve yourself!

Of course, a few brave females will often just say "screw it" and invade the men's room. Men enjoy this. They believe the defeated kidney must acquiesce to the Kingdom of Many Urinals. The women get the added humiliation of smiles and jeers to heap onto the indignity they have been feeling for the last ten minutes standing in a line that looks like a scene from "Hands Across America."

Occasionally, the police are summoned, and they saunter into the men's room to arrest the trespassing women. Of course, the warrant should go out to the people who design these inadequate facilities: the planners, the architects, the contractors, the plumbers. Hmmm. Could there be a common thread here? Let's see, when was the last time your toilet backed up and the plumber was a woman? When was the last time the contractor or builder had the double X chromosome?

The fact is, there are few female builders, contractors, and plumbers, so it is little wonder that those behind the decision that leads to women standing in line have never had to stand in a line.

We called up an architect and a plumber and asked them why they never design and build enough women's toilets. This is a compilation of what we were told:

"There's no getting around it—women just take longer than men in the rest room and that's why they have a longer line. They've got to undo their dress, they unsnap their garters, they pull down the panty hose, then the panties, then sit down. Men just whip it out and go! Then when women are done, they fuss around the mirror, reapplying their lipstick, fixing their eye shadow, and generally taking their sweet time. And they like to talk to each other. A man has got nothing to say to the other men at the urinal. It's just in and out."

Makes sense doesn't it . . . guys?

In the end, it all comes down to the other bottom line: It costs more money to build toilets and stalls than it does to build urinals. So the women must wait.

We felt that during a time of reduced feminism (which, admittedly, is caused in part by some feminists not addressing the issues of the working class), instead of taking a stand for some abstract political issue it would be good to stand up for something so basic, so common, that every woman would applaud our political movement. We

The Johns of Justice roll across the country.

decided to stand up for the right of every woman to pee, to pee whenever she wanted to and as quickly as she wanted to.

We rented a flatbed truck and a half-dozen Port-O-Sans and created the Johns of Justice. Our goal: to let women relieve themselves with pride and dignity—and no wait.

The Johns of Justice, with *TV Nation* correspondent Karen Duffy behind the wheel, roamed the streets of the cities of America, stopping by concert halls, baseball stadiums, cinemas, and Broadway theaters, announcing to the women inside that they did not have to wait—THEY COULD GO RIGHT HERE AND NOW!

On her bullhorn, Karen implored:

> Women and girls
> Don't be meek—
> Climb aboard and
> Take a leak!

and,

> Give me a P(ee)!

Karen Duffy waves to the crowds.

We even wrote our own anthem, "The Johns of Justice" (see page 147), and sang it wherever we went.

By the dozens, women left the lines of indignity and poured out on the street to use our clean, well-lit, fragrant portable toilets. They were exuberant. Liberated. And, on their way out, they received a free hot towel from Karen.

The Johns of Justice certainly made a dent and an impression, but there is more to this story.

In many workplaces, the issue of the lack of women's facilities has resulted in numerous health hazards and, in some cases, women losing their jobs.

At the Pro Line ball cap company near Dallas, Texas, the Occupational Safety and Health Administration (OSHA) had

cited the company for not having enough women's rest rooms. Pro Line assessed their predicament and decided that it was cheaper to fire all of the women than to build another ladies' room. This resulted in the Equal Employment Opportunity Commission (EEOC), the federal watchdog for civil rights that itself is poorly staffed and underfunded, to file suit against Pro Line.

When we visited and interviewed some of the women who had been fired, they shared with us their fight to gain the most basic of rights. They explained to us that while there were approximately 150 women working at Pro Line and only about six men, there was an equal number of rest rooms: one for each gender. Pro Line blamed the firings on OSHA.

We took the Johns of Justice to Dallas and pulled into the parking lot of Pro Line. Karen announced to them that we were now providing the toilets that they wouldn't, free of charge. Right away, management called the cops. Within minutes, the police arrived and threatened to arrest the crew and Karen and confiscate the toilets. Karen explained to them who the real culprits were, and they

Karen tells the cop that she's "just gotta go."

The Johns of Justice

Words and Music by Jay Martel

A mighty rig came rumblin'
On down the interstate
With diesel engines gunnin'
And five Port-O-Sans as freight.
Salvation to each woman
Who can't heed nature's call,
Here come the Johns of Justice
Relieving one and all.

The pedal's to the metal
'Cause you know they've got a
    date,
Speedin' past the smokies
'Cause there's women who
    can't wait.
Wherever there are victims
of potty prejudice,
Here come the Johns of Justice
Rollin' through the mist.

Yipee-ki-yay!
Floosh!
Yipee-ki-yay!
Floosh!

When Pro Line canned their
    women
Instead of building cans,

When Nabisco told their sisters
To go only on demand,
Whenever they eliminate
Elimination sites,
Here come the Johns of Justice
Flushing wrongs a-right.

Spoken solemnly:
In every town there's a theater
Where women wait in line,
While men go when they please
In a fraction of the time.
It's time for all to stand up
For those who can't sit down,
Here come the Johns of Justice
Drivin' into town.

Here come the Johns of Justice
Leave that seat on down.

*Spoken as the music fades
    out:*
Just leave that old thing right
where it is, boys. Leave it down.
Got to do the right thing you
know. Just don't move it at all.
I told you. You don't know what
it's like being a woman.

seemed sympathetic, but they stated that we had violated the sacred rule of "private property." They then issued a second warning, and the Johns of Justice pulled away.

Next, we heard about a canning company in Oxnard, California, where the women were not let off the assembly line to relieve themselves, so, naturally, we were off to the Golden State. Eight workers filed federal sex discrimination complaints accusing Nabisco Foods of not letting them use the bathroom, other than during breaks, while men were allowed to go whenever they wanted. Some women had developed bladder infections and others began wearing diapers to work.

We pulled our Johns of Justice onto the property of the plant and, true to form, the police were called. Again, we were threatened with arrest. But this time one of the officers was a woman and, well, let's just say that sisterhood is pretty powerful when it comes to Number One. The female cop had a hard time holding back her smile, and we gave her a "Johns of Justice" ball cap and T-shirt. We then left, but not without warning the managers to "Let Your Women GO!"

So next time you see the line of women snaking down a corridor because some man chose not to install enough toilets, just step right up to the front and lead them all in a joyous chorus of "The Johns of Justice!"

20

With Neighbors Like These

When they hauled Jeffrey Dahmer out of his Milwaukee apartment for having butchered and partially eaten sixteen human beings, the neighbors all remarked what a nice boy he seemed to be. No, they never did notice that fifty-five-gallon drum he was carrying into his home. Didn't smell any of the rotting flesh either. The cops thought nothing of it when a fourteen-year-old boy came running naked and screaming out of Jeff's apartment; in fact, they returned the boy to Dahmer so he could later finish off the kid's execution.

This is how it always is. The police capture a serial killer and the neighbors act totally surprised. The most they ever say is that he may have seemed "a little strange" or that "he kept to himself."

John Wayne Gacy buried twenty-seven kids under the floorboards of his house. Sure, the neighbors heard the chainsaw at three in the morning, but, hey, this is America and goddammit, you've got the right to chop some wood at 3:00 A.M. without anyone getting into your business.

Joel Rifkin left for work at 8:00 A.M. carrying body bags out of his house. No one seemed to notice. The neighbors probably figured he had a big project happening at the office. John Esposito kept little Katie alive underground in a bunker he dug in his backyard, and the most the neighbors ever thought was that it was nice to see him out doing some yard work.

Today, the FBI estimates that there are close to one hundred serial killers operating in the U.S. One may be living next to you. But how would you know? Ask yourself this—do you even know who lives next door to you? How about the people two doors down from you—what do they do for a living? What are their kids' names? It wasn't that long ago when we all grew up in neighborhoods where you could name every single person on the block—you knew them personally and had a relationship with them.

These days, that is no longer the case. We do whatever we can to avoid the neighbors. We don't want to know who they are because we're so damn tired when we come home from work we want to be just left the hell alone. Need to borrow a cup of sugar? Go to the freakin' 7-Eleven!

To test our theory that no one would know if a serial killer was living in their neighborhood—and if they had any suspicions would do absolutely nothing about it—we went out to Westbury, Long Island. There, we rented a house in a nice suburban neighborhood and hired an actor who looked like a dad on *Home Improvement.*

We then set about having our actor do every horrific thing all the top serial killers do. We equipped him with hacksaws, axes, pickaxes, bomb-making manuals, and women's clothing. He buried not one but ten fifty-five-gallon drums in the front and backyard. He operated power tools at two in the morning. He fired off a shotgun at four in the morning. Bloodstains appeared everywhere inside and on the exterior of the house.

As he did these things, nobody paid him the time of day. He switched his mailbox number to 666 and no one cared, not even the mailman. He played loud satanic music. He paced back and forth in the house, letting out howls. He put fake blood on a mattress and left it at the curb for the garbage truck to pick up. No one noticed, no one cared. Only a neighborhood dog stopped to sniff the mattress, sensing trouble. But his master paid him no heed and walked on.

Days of this went by, and the cozy little bedroom community just kept on humming, the people unaware of our man's activities.

When the week ended, we decided to up the ante. Our guy hung a big sheet on his front porch announcing a "Kids Only Picnic" on Saturday at 1:00 P.M.—no parents allowed. We were

sure that would do the trick but, surprisingly, no one called the cops.

Finally, on Sunday, we sent our guest correspondent, Jonathan Katz, around to the neighbors to ask if they had seen anything strange over at 666. Most of the neighbors admitted they had noticed something going on but chose to ignore it because they didn't think it was right to pry into someone else's lifestyle. One neighbor did say she called the cops because she heard loud, spooky music, but the police never arrived and she just dropped it.

After we told the people in the neighborhood what had transpired, they became very angry at us. The city of Westbury hired a lawyer to sue us for "emotional duress." When Jim Czarnecki, the producer of the piece, had to go back to the house to wrap things up, he encountered some very hostile neighbors. He cleaned the place and got out as quickly as he could.

To smooth things over, our supervising producer, Jerry Kupfer, went out to Westbury, had cocktails with the neighbors, and tried to explain our point of view. Most understood, and those who didn't received a crisp $100 bill for having the bejesus scared out of them.

NBC thought the piece was truly sick and considered not airing it. They finally agreed to show it, but we had to cut the "Kid's Picnic" notice out of the story. We also had to dump the idea of tying a goat up in the yard to be used as a sacrifice. Fear of the animal activists put the kibosh to that. Frankly, you would think fear of Satanists who might be upset at us for mocking their religion would be even worse, but let us assure you there is no fear of Lucifer at the network owned by the men of General Electric.

A few years later, director Quentin Tarantino let us know that "Neighbors" was his favorite *TV Nation* segment and, for us, that made not being able to behead the goat a lot easier to take.

21

Health Care Olympics

Forty million Americans have absolutely no health care, but who gives an enema? Wall Street is healthy and that's all that matters!

Other countries look at this statistic and are appalled. You talk to any Canadian, Brit, German, or Kenyan and they cannot comprehend that our national health policy is: "You're sick? Too bad!"

What's almost worse is that those with health care are being forced to pay outrageous sums of money for belonging to an HMO ("Hand the Money Over"). With an HMO, you don't get help—you get referred.

Meanwhile, the executives at these HMOs are becoming filthy rich. In 1996, the head of U.S. Healthcare pulled in nearly one billion dollars in compensation for himself. That's right, one *billion*.

So is it any wonder that the U.S. places twenty-third among the nations of the world in infant mortality? We can send a dozen battleships to the Persian Gulf in a matter of hours, but if you're worried that your kid's sore throat is developing into something worse, well, take a number and prepare to sit in an emergency room filled with gunshot victims for a very long time.

To hear our congressmen tell it—the very congressmen who have refused to do anything about health care in the two terms of the Health Care President—our health systems are in fine shape, light-years ahead of every other country. The only problems, they tell us, are: (1) welfare people who suck up too many tax dollars by having the arrogance to get sick, and (2) lawyers who sue negligent doctors.

We do like to think of ourselves as Number One, so we decided to pit our health-care system against the systems of Canada and Cuba. We called it the "Health Care Olympics" and thought it would be interesting to follow one patient with a broken bone from the moment he or she entered the emergency room to the moment he or she got the bill from the hospital. One patient from Canada, one patient from Cuba, and one from the home team, the good old U.S.A.

We asked sportscasters Bob Costas and Ahmad Rashad to cover the play-by-play. In our New York studio, they followed the action

Bob Costas and Ahmad Rashad, hosts of the TV Nation Health Care Olympics.

Team Canada: Sunnybrook Health Science Center.

in the three hospitals to see which health-care system would win the gold in the first-ever televised *TV Nation* Health Care Olympics.

Let's join Costas and Rashad with the games already under way:

BOB COSTAS: The countries: the U.S., Canada, and Cuba. The health-care systems: free enterprise, government-paid, and socialist. The challenge: legs, ankles, and feet. Tonight these teams of some of the best health-care professionals in the world face off for another evening of grueling competition in the *TV Nation* Health Care Olympics.

In the U.S. watch the team in Florida face the obstacles of a private insurance-driven system in order to maintain America's position as a world leader in research and technology.

AMERICAN DOCTOR: I think we do a great job in America, we're really cutting edge.

COSTAS: Then in Toronto, Ontario, will Canada continue to score big with the access and simplicity of universal coverage?

CANADIAN NURSE: They can come without having to worry about paying for anything.

COSTAS: And in Havana, Cuba. Can this third-world republic continue to remain competitive with the medical powers of the industrialized world in the face of severe economic strain?

CUBAN NURSE: This is a very good system.

COSTAS: Good evening, everybody, I'm Bob Costas. Another exciting day as three countries were poised for the global challenge in today's lower limb competition. Now joining me today in our *TV Nation* coverage is my long-time colleague Ahmad Rashad.

AHMAD RASHAD: Thanks a lot, Bob. Now you know anytime two very strong government-based systems and one solid market-based system lock horns, excitement is always guaranteed, and today was no exception.

COSTAS: I'll say. What criteria were the judges mainly looking at?

RASHAD: Well the ER performances were evaluated on the ADCs of health care: **Access, Delivery, and Cost.**

COSTAS: Alright, so let's track the action as it began here in the U.S. where security was tight and a sideline gang got things started with a cheer.

U.S. EMERGENCY ROOM TEAM: U.S. is number one!

COSTAS: The venue was Broward General in Florida, where the patient entered without any assistance and took a seat ready and waiting for the next step.

RASHAD: Bob, what's interesting here is that long waits are typically more characteristic of Canada with rationing of services due to limited resources. But as you can see, the patient at Sunnybrook Health Science Center in Ontario practically sailed through the check-in process.

COSTAS: And down in Cuba, at Colesto General, the patient, as you see, arrived in an ambulance, signaling a higher degree of difficulty in his injury.

RASHAD: That's exactly right, Bob. Also if we can get an instant replay here you can see that the patient came to the emergency room with a temporary cast and a set of X-rays already. That's because he had been to see his family doctor first.

Costas: Back in the U.S. the patient went through triage, a way of prioritizing treatment according to severity. Whereas in Cuba the patient was immediately surrounded by team activity. No triage necessary.

After check-in, the patients in Canada and the U.S. were exiled to a sort of waiting-area limbo.

Rashad: Not necessarily a bad place to be, Bob, because as you can see some of the players even managed to provide care in the hallways.

Costas: Sure, but wasn't that ankle more vulnerable there than if the patient would have been waiting in a cubicle like the patient in the U.S.?

Rashad: Vulnerable indeed when an innocent bystander added insult to the injury by running into the injured patient's leg. Now, if you take another look at this instant replay you'll see the unintentional bump—RIGHT THERE! OOH! Luckily, there was no additional damage done but nevertheless quite a tense moment there at Sunnybrook.

Costas: And it is a good thing he was headed for X-rays just like his counterparts in Cuba and the U.S. Things are really heating up. Ahmad, how do you sum up the first half of action?

Rashad: Well, Bob, we saw the United States really struggle when it came to access to medical care. But that's one area in which the Americans are always at a severe disadvantage because of the forty million citizens here who are uninsured. Now in terms of delivery, all three countries admitted their patients with relatively equal speed and efficiency.

Costas: Thankfully for Canada, waiting lists don't factor into the emergency competition. For other procedures, though, Canadians may find themselves waiting for months due to limited budgets. Now America should be able to pick up some ground with its superior technology and equipment. Cuba, on the other hand, may be vulnerable in the second half because the thirty-three-year embargo against this island nation coupled with the absence of Soviet sponsorship has made certain medicines and basic supplies scarce.

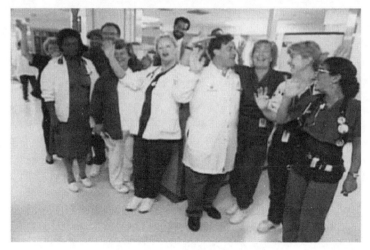

Team U.S.A.: Broward General in Florida.

RASHAD: But Cuba is sure to pick up a big advantage in the cost category with no charges to the patients at all. And Canada, well, they're also a strong contender in this category, with just about all costs covered.

COSTAS: How do you think the coaches felt about their teams' first-half performances?

RASHAD: It was very interesting. All three seemed pretty optimistic. Here's some of what they had to say:

WIL TROWER (U.S.A.): I wouldn't necessarily say I'm *the* coach. I'm one of them.

JOSE LARA TUNON (CUBA): Health-care costs nothing to the patient because health is a right to our citizens.

PETER ELLIS, CEO OF SUNNYBROOK (CANADA): When 30 percent of the provincial budget is spent on health care you become a very easy and vulnerable target as governments try to get their deficits in line.

WIL TROWER (U.S.A.): There are a number of teams, as you can imagine, in an organization as large and complex as this and we do try to work together collaboratively and provide the support.

COSTAS: And we near the end of halftime with a fine view of the Cuban venue from the *TV Nation* blimp. Thanks for the shot, guys. Those fellows do work hard. Should be an interesting second half, Ahmad.

RASHAD: You bet, Bob.

COSTAS: Now back to the action. The radiologists and doctors took a closer look and found a hairline fracture in Canada, a bad sprain in the U.S. And a flat-out broken leg in Cuba.

RASHAD: We caught up with the team in Cuba after the bone-setting operation for a "post-op" locker-room interview.

RAFAEL PIORNO FERMOSELLE, M.D.: I am totally satisfied with having succeeded once more in fulfilling the task of resolving a problem with the human body.

COSTAS: In the final stretch our clock showed that the industrialized nation patients had more wait time before their casts were put on with total precast waiting time in Canada 2:15:00 . . .

. . . and 1:15:00 in the U.S.

Meanwhile team Cuba made sure their young patient came out OK. Keep in mind that unlike the others he did have a broken leg and therefore needed an operation to set the bone, but as you can see it was a big success for Colesto General.

RASHAD: The Canadian team relied heavily on the star performance of one doctor through the casting process, with the team members at the U.S. venue showing proficiency as well. Ultimately all countries got their patients up and on their way.

COSTAS: Man—that was exhilarating action—almost like you're right there.

RASHAD: Tremendous footage.

COSTAS: I'd definitely second that.

Well the scores came in and as we anticipated it all came down to the big "C"—*cost.*

In Cuba . . .

DOCTOR: The patient pays nothing.

COSTAS: In Canada . . .

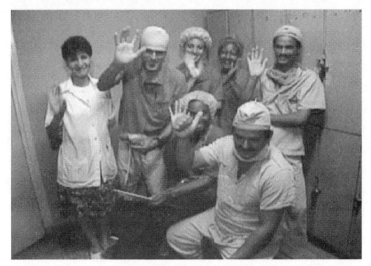

Team Cuba: Colestro General.

NURSE: Fifteen dollars for the crutches he just received—that is it.

COSTAS: And in the U.S. . . .

HOSPITAL ADMINISTRATOR: The patient will be charged $80 for an emergency room service visit; foot X-ray, $137; Ace bandage, $44; X-ray of the ankle, $118; $16.90, dye used in the X-ray process; adult crutches, $46. Total charges for the service: $450.70.

RASHAD: Unfortunately it may take a while for the U.S. to make its way through the insurance obstacle, and who knows what can happen with reform, but always a solid performer, it placed third. Cuba had some really great moments and wins points for such a comprehensive medical system but until they find a way out of economic isolation it's going to be hard to sustain the quality of their system. Cuba placed second.

COSTAS: But it was our neighbor to the north who stood strong with over twenty years of universal access, they take the lower limb gold in '94. Yes, team Canada, seen here waving the flag of victory as another night in the *TV Nation* Health Care Olympics comes to a close.

Now a disclaimer. The competition applied to lower limb injuries only. Who knows the outcome if we were talking gall bladders, tonsillectomy, or liposuction. Thanks again. I'm Bob Costas.

RASHAD: And, I'm Ahmad Rashad. Good night.

TOGETHER: And good health.

As you know, *TV Nation* was a nonfiction, documentary show. While we used humor and created situations to illustrate our own point of view, everything seen on the show was recorded as it actually happened.

Except here. For the first and only time on *TV Nation*, NBC censors made us change the ending of a segment. The truth is, by applying the standards of the competition fairly to each country, Cuba won. It provided the best care in the fastest time and for absolutely no fee to the patient. The censor told us that politically there was no way we could show Cuba winning on primetime television. We were told to make Canada the winner. We argued right up to show time that this was both dishonest and also pretty silly. Did NBC think that a new missile crisis would erupt if we showed the commies winning? Did they fear a new set of Boat People—but this time with hundreds of Americans sailing to Cuba for decent, affordable health care?

We lost, and the piece aired with Canada as the winner. It makes you wonder what else is "changed" on TV if something this insignificant cannot even make it on the air in its original form.

22

Cobb County

In November of 1994, the Republicans took
over both houses of Congress with Newt Gingrich as their leader.
They ran on a platform of dismantling the federal government and
virtually hating everything it stood for. They promised to cut federal spending to the bone, starting with welfare and other programs they viewed as part of the liberal agenda.

There were, of course, two problems with this. One, the Republicans were responsible for driving up the national debt by a whopping $3 trillion during the Reagan and Bush years. So, expecting
them to cut spending was like expecting Gore to be president in the
year 2000. It just isn't going to happen.

And two, the American people actually like their government.
When the Republicans tried to shut down all the federal offices in
late 1995, the public reacted strongly. The people know that the federal government is that Social Security check being delivered on the
first of the month, the student loan office sending out the college
funds, and the air traffic control system making sure Grandma's
plane home doesn't crash into Mount St. Helens. Yes, it turned out

that we, the people, don't hate the federal government after all—a serious miscalculation on the part of the Republicans. Their undoing was complete when in Oklahoma City the federal building was blown up in a fit of "I hate the federal government" rage. The ugly tone the Republicans had set had its logical conclusion in the rubble of the Murrah Building with its 168 dead.

But this did not stop Newt Gingrich and his anti-Washington rhetoric. So it was time to give him the *TV Nation* treatment.

With a little bit of research (thanks to *Common Cause* magazine) we discovered that Newt's district of Cobb County, Georgia, received more federal funds than any other suburban county in the country, with the exception of Arlington, Virginia (home of the Pentagon) and Broward County, Florida (home of Cape Canaveral).

That's right, nearly $4 billion a year of our hard-earned tax money was going to a guy who hated getting it! So, we figured, if Newt couldn't stand the sight of federal funds, then the least he could do was give it back to the federal government. Let him set an example for the rest of the country by cutting waste at home first.

We flew down to Cobb County and opened up an office for a new organization that would help Newt return the evil money to D.C. We called our group GOBAC—Get Government Off Our Backs. We then quickly identified those items Newt's constituents in Cobb County were getting for free and what it cost us taxpayers:

Senior Citizens Centers	$261,000
Railroad warning lights	$74,000
Marijuana research at Kennesaw State College	$600,000
Libraries	$22,000
Sewage treatment	$6,000,000
Police car bumpers	$2,100
Chiropractic colleges	$270,000
Lake Allatoona	$350,000
Lockheed	$3,000,000,000

Mike explores landlocked Cobb County.

It was an astounding list considering the potholes that sit unfixed in the streets where you live, not to mention the forty million Americans without health care and the dismal ranking our schools have—the lowest among Western nations.

One of GOBAC's first actions was to enter the annual Fourth of July parade in Marietta, Georgia, the seat of Cobb County. The high point of the parade was none other than the congressman himself, Newton Leroy Gingrich, marching along with his supporters.

Before the parade Mike had a chance to talk to Newt and thank him for trying to cut government spending. Newt liked that. Mike asked him what government fat he would like to start cutting in Cobb County. Newt said he'd have to think about that. But Mike had a list. He whipped out a piece of paper that detailed all the money Cobb gets from Washington and started to suggest some cuts.

"How about Lockheed?" Mike asked.

"If you're gonna downsize systems, I think you oughta retrain them," Newt responded.

"How about school lunches?"

"I favor *increasing* the money for school lunches."

Increase? We thought Newt wanted to *cut* spending. He was going in the wrong direction.

"How about this $17,000 for the Coast Guard?" Mike asked. "Where's the coast? You're landlocked here!"

Newt gave Mike the evil eye and called an end to the interview. His aides rushed him away.

Mike took this rejection personally, and decided to catch up with Newt in the parade. Waiting until Newt and his cheering section came into view, he stepped out into the street and marched along with them, uninvited.

Starting at the back of the pack of Newties in the parade, Mike slowly inched his way forward to the front, where Gingrich was in command. Suddenly, before Newt knew what hit him, there was Mike walking right along with him, waving and smiling to the crowd in unison with Newt.

Gingrich became instantly annoyed. He leaned over to Mike and said, "I have to warn you, there's a sharpshooter up there on the roof pointing a gun at you."

Mike looked across the street to the rooftops and, sure enough, there was a man in a uniform pointing a gun with a scope, aiming at him.

"I have no desire to die so that the Fox Network can get a forty share," Mike told Newt in a voice that indicated he suddenly needed an adult diaper. Mike quickly dropped out of the Newt section of the parade.

Further back was Congressman Bob Barr, whose district adjoins Newt's. Mike popped back into the parade (there were no sharpshooters protecting Representative Barr, as he was a freshman congressman and a pain in the ass). He asked Barr how he felt about the federal deficit. Barr said we should slash and burn wherever possible. What would you cut in your district? Barr was silent. Could you do with a billion less? More silence. Barr contin-

ued waving and walking away from Mike, ignoring his simple questions.

As we walked along we handed out flyers to the crowd watching the parade, telling them how they could give back that filthy federal money. We flew a plane above the parade with a banner that read: GET FEDERAL $$ OUT OF COBB NOW! We handed out bumper stickers that read: IF YOU CAN READ THIS—YOU'RE TAKING TOO MUCH GOVERNMENT $$$. Mike used a megaphone to thank the crowd for giving the country Newt Gingrich and that now we wanted to show our thanks by taking back all the federal money that Cobb County felt so burdened by.

Before long, the crowd started to turn on us. Some started to boo. Parade organizers came by and physically removed our signs from us. Finally, we were asked to leave.

We heard that the local Republicans were holding a Fourth of July barbecue after the parade, so we drove over and talked our way in. There, the meat-eating conservatives gave us interview after interview about how welfare needed to be abolished. But no one

No, you're not hallucinating.

seemed to think that the welfare *they* were getting should be touched.

Then, to our surprise, in walked Newt Gingrich. He spotted us immediately and cried, "Oh, no, not you again!" We promised that we would leave him alone as long as he did a promo for our show. Before he had a chance to think about it, Mike grabbed his hand in a shake, looked directly into the camera, and said, "No, you're not hallucinating, I'm Michael Moore, this is Newt Gingrich, and tonight on *TV Nation*, Newt and Mike save America."

Newt was like a deer caught in headlights. His forced smile as he took Mike's direction and looked into the camera said it all: "GET ME THE HELL OUT OF HERE!" But it was too late.

Having failed to convince Newt to help him save his own Republican Revolution, Mike had no choice but to go out and do it himself. Come hell or high water, Mike was going to see that the budget would get balanced and that Cobb County would lead the way.

GOBAC closes down I-75.

First, Mike tried to convince all the workers at Lockheed to go home for the day so that federal funds would not be spent on building weapons America didn't need anyway. As he stood at the main gate, Mike sadly had no takers for his effort.

Next, he tried to shut down the local stretch of the interstate. "Don't use this federal highway," he pleaded to motorists at the beginning of an entrance ramp to I-75. "It's built by evil Washington money!" Cars whizzed right over the cones he had placed to block their entrance.

Then it was off to try and shut down the library. "Don't read these books," he asked the patrons inside. "This library was built by bureaucrats in the District of Columbia. Send those books back!" But people just kept on reading.

No matter where he went, Mike could not find a single Cobb County resident who would stop using the things that were provided to them free of charge by the federal government. "Why don't you just start with someone else?" one man asked him at the library. "Take it from the other guy, that's what it's all about, isn't it?"

He was right. Let the other guy go without while *he's* paying your way. The American Way.

It was clear that the people who gave us Newt didn't really detest the federal government after all.

Back in New York, we completed our story and sent it off to the Fox Network. The executives for the show were mortified. That was the time when the press was full of stories about Rupert Murdoch and Newt's book deal. (Not long after that, representatives of News Corporation [Murdoch's parent company which owns Harper-Collins, the original publisher of both this book and Newt's book] testified before the U.S. House Standards Committee that Murdoch had nothing to do with the book deal and the Committee ruled that there was no impropriety about the deal.) In any event, the executives said no to the piece.

For three weeks, Mike argued back and forth with the network, trying to negotiate a solution. Finally, we were told that the executives on the show thought this was a hot potato and they didn't want to touch it. The piece was dead. Over. Gone.

The next day, Mike did not show up to work. He didn't come in for three days. The *TV Nation* staff were beginning to wonder what was going on. The executives at Columbia TriStar wanted to know why their calls were not being returned.

Finally, Mike told the studio that he was quitting the show. By that evening the network called to say that they had changed their minds, "Cobb County" could air. Mike thanked them and went back to work.

Although the executives for the show insisted that the piece not lead that week's show, and instead be buried somewhere in the second half hour, it was a big hit with our audience and resulted in a lot of positive mail to Fox.

A few months later, we received a call from the Flint congressman, Dale Kildee. He had just come from a meeting on Capitol

*GOBAC, in association with the Cobb County Chapter
of Govaholics Anonymous, presents:*

The Twelve Steps to Overcoming Federal-Money Dependency

1. I admit that I am addicted to federal funds and that, partly as a result, our federal budget has become unmanageable.
2. The problem is not welfare mothers, the "urban" areas, food stamps, or the NEA. The problem is me.
3. I believe that by recognizing my addiction to government money, I am making a big step toward getting government off my back.
4. I am ready to make a searching and fearless inventory of all the federal money and services I am presently using.
5. Only by immediately ceasing the use of all federal funds and services can I hope to break myself of these cravings.
6. I will no longer accept federal pensions, jobs paid for with federal money, federal housing loans, federal anything.
7. I will no longer drive on federal roads, accept federal delivery of mail, or picnic with my family in federally funded parks.
8. I trust in God to give me the ability to stop the federal spending I can, accept the federal spending I can't, and help me to know the difference.
9. I have made a list of all persons that I've harmed from excessive use of federal funds and services—including my sons and daughters, who will never get a decent Social Security check—and have asked for their forgiveness.
10. I will continue to use vigilance to ensure that not so much as a single federally funded toothpick enters my mouth.
11. Since U.S. currency is also paid for with federal funds, I will now give up all that I possess to this fine organization.
12. Having made my own spiritual awakening, I will now carry this message to other federal money addicts here in Cobb County, including Lockheed employees, Coast Guard officers, and congressional representatives. Amen.

Hill of the top Democratic members of Congress, where the "Cobb County" segment featuring Newt Gingrich was shown to all assembled.

"You wouldn't believe the reaction in the room," Kildee told us. "The whole place was cheering. We have all been feeling defeated since the Republicans took over both houses. This lifted our spirits considerably. It was the first laugh we've had in a long time. Then Dick Gephardt (the Democratic leader) gave an inspiring speech that it was time to pick ourselves up and get back into the fight. Thanks, guys, for doing that story."

If You Can Read This... **YOU'RE TAKING TOO MUCH GOVERNMENT $$$**

23

Making Peace with Pizza

They've been fighting in Bosnia since A.D. 1054. In this decade alone, a quarter million people have been killed. In 1994, when *TV Nation* was on NBC, the leading nightly news reports were (1) Bosnia, (2) Bosnia, and (3) Bosnia. It seemed natural that one segment on *TV Nation* should address this issue, so we approached the network about it.

"No!" came the plea back from the "Must See TV" network. "Bosnia is ratings suicide."

"Yeah, but that's why *we* should do it," we replied. "Maybe the reason everyone tunes out Bosnia is because no one in this country understands what is going on over there. Maybe *we* can explain it. Maybe *we* could make it more compelling."

"I will bet you $100 that the ratings will drop minute by minute during the entire piece," one executive challenged us. (They can actually monitor ratings nationwide on a second-by-second basis.)

"Okay, you're on."

Our idea was simple: go to meet with the ambassadors from the warring parties—the Serbs and the Croats—and get them to sit down, eat pizza together, and sing songs.

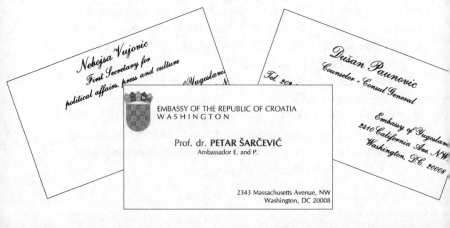

Our producer, Joanne Doroshow, went to Washington, D.C., and convinced both the Yugoslavian consulate general (the Serbs insist on calling their country Yugoslavia, even though it does not resemble the former Yugoslavia) and the Croatian ambassador to meet with Mike.

A little background:

The Serbs, the Croats, and the Muslims all claim to own Bosnia. The Muslims are the majority but have had little power over the years. During World War II the Croats and the Muslims sided with Hitler and together slaughtered 500,000 Serbs. But in the 1990s, the tables turned. The Serbs have slaughtered about 200,000 Muslims since 1992, while the Croats were way off their game, killing only 20,000 Serbs and Muslims.

As a cultural gesture, we drove over to see the Serbs in an old Yugo, truly the worst car humans ever built. We thought they would like that, and they did. The embassy staff all rushed out to take a look under the hood and give the tires a kick. Fortunately, nothing fell off the car.

Mike wonders why the Serbs are blue.

We listened to their version of why they had to murder 200,000 people. This *was* TV and we wanted to at least do what they do on TV news and give an illusion of fairness. But in reality we had our minds made up. We couldn't shoot an objective story at all because we don't usually feel objective about governments who believe in killing that many people.

The Serbian political liaison, Nebojsa Vujovic, took Michael on a tour of the embassy. Michael wondered what territories the Serbs believed rightfully belonged to them. Mr. Vujovic pulled out a map and pointed out the areas. They were all shaded in blue. After chatting for a while, Vujovic talked about his personal interests—his favorite TV show was *Murder, She Wrote,* and his favorite song was Dylan's "Knockin' on Heaven's Door." (In case you were wondering—NO, we do not write anyone's lines on *TV Nation.* This is a documentary show.)

We ordered a pizza for lunch and when we sat down to eat, the Serbian consulate general, Dušan Paunovic, joined us. He was a jovial guy, and when Michael asked if he would pretend that the pizza was the former Yugoslavia, he agreed. Then Michael handed

Mr. Paunovic helps himself to a slice of Slovenia.

Mr. Vujovic a big knife and asked him to carve up the pizza as he saw fit. Happily, he complied.

"This piece is Croatia," he explained as he carved off a tiny piece of the pizza. "This is Serbia." He cut a huge piece off. "And this is Bosnia, consisting of three ingredients: ham is for the Croats, pepperoni is the Muslims, and the cheese is Serbia."

Michael lifted out the slice of Bosnia and generously handed it to Mr. Paunovic. "Here, eat a slice of Bosnia."

"No, no, that's too much," he protested. "But I would like a piece of Slovenia," he added, and he reached for the knife and lopped off a slice of the pizza. "My mother, you see, she was from Slovenia."

Right then, Mike asked him if he would like to call up the Croat ambassador and invite him over for some of the pizza. "No, we do not call them first," he firmly answered. "They can call us."

The Serbs went along with everything Michael asked, and while they may have thought he was a little strange, they never stopped him or said anything negative about the meeting. We left on excellent terms.

Mike got back in the Yugo and headed over to see the Croats. He hoped that they would be a bit more amenable and maybe willing to take the first step to ending this bitter conflict.

They were not. They had their own map of who owned what in the former Yugoslavia, and of course their share was bigger on their map than it had been on the Serbs'. And their territories were also marked in blue.

"Hey, you both can't have blue," Mike told Petar Šarčević, the Croatian ambassador. But Petar insisted that the Croats were the only ones who had the right to claim blue as their color.

Mike was determined to bring the two sides together. He proposed an idea. Through the magic of editing, they could appear on camera, side by side, and sing a song to each other. The Croat and the Serb agreed, and each sang out the Barney song. It was a beautiful moment, worthy of a prize from the United Nations.

Mike leads Petar in a rousing rendition of the Barney song.

"I love you.
You love me.
We're a happy fam-i-ly

It was hard to believe that there was a dry eye across America when this segment aired. The ratings never went down and we never got our hundred bucks. Why the two representatives from these countries agreed to do this is anyone's guess.

After it aired, the Serbs issued a formal protest to NBC. But they did not back up their threats with any attempts at mass slaughter of our staff. Wimps.

24

We Hire Our Own Lobbyist

Every corporation, every industry group, every right-wing cause (and a few liberal ones, too), has its own lobbyist in Washington, D.C. From the National Snack Foods Association to the American Mushroom Institute to the National Pork Board, it seems everyone has an office near Capitol Hill looking out for its best interests—which rarely coincide with *our* best interests. Men and women in tailored suits stalk the halls of Congress, making sure that the bills that will exempt them from pollution laws, give them tax breaks for their company yacht, or reward them with subsidies to help them build a factory in Indonesia are passed quickly and quietly so that most of the time none of us will be hip to what is going on.

Millions of dollars fund this process every year. Millions, that is, that go into the pockets of congressmen and senators. Our democracy has been hijacked by those with the most money. We can't get national health care, or free college, or safer workplaces, or universal child care because *we* don't have the funds to buy the votes.

We got to thinking—what if we did have some money? Could we get something done in our nation's capital, something that would benefit the people for once instead of the rich guys? Let's say we had $5,000. Just how much democracy can you buy for $5,000?

We decided to give it a try.

Armed with the network's cold hard cash—and a few "souvenirs" to hand out to our elected officials—we headed down to Washington, D.C., to see if we could get a law passed that would benefit *us*.

First, we figured we needed a registered lobbyist. We looked in the Yellow Pages and found just the guy. Bill Chasey ran his own lobbying firm just a few blocks from the Capitol Building. He seemed well connected, and all the congressmen we met seemed to know him. He was

Bill Chasey, lobbyist.

personable, had a good sense of humor, and, most important for us, he would get us some legislation for a mere $5,000.

We told Bill that we wanted a law passed, an amendment to the IRS code that would give a tax break to "anyone who worked on a television program known as *TV Nation.*" Because we do believe in paying our fare share of the tax load, we were kindly requesting only a 50 percent tax reduction in our federal income taxes.

Bill told us that it would be difficult to obtain such a large break, that most congressmen would want to know, "Why should we give a 50 percent tax break to the crew of *TV Nation*?"

We told him to tell them, "Because they paid me five grand, dammit, and it's my job to get them what they want!"

Bill explained that the lobbying profession didn't quite work like that. We would have to give the congressmen something, too—including a more rational reason for the tax reduction. Bill told us the members of Congress would ask, "Why not give it to everyone, not just *TV Nation* employees?"

What a good idea!

"But," Bill responded, "it's going to cost a lot more than $5,000 to get a bill like that passed."

Well, five thousand is all NBC would give us to "convince" congressmen to give us our own line in the tax code.

Bill had another idea.

"Why not consider asking Congress for your own nationally recognized day?"

"You mean one day each year that would be known as '*TV Nation* Day'?"

"Exactly! It happens all the time."

Hmmm. *TV Nation* Day. It did have a nice ring to it. The thought of citizens across America celebrating one sacred day in our honor with parades, picnics, and half-off sales at Wal-Mart made our hearts proud and our heads swell. *TV Nation* Day—just what the country needed during times like these. We told Bill to go for it.

We decided that August 16 should be declared the official *TV Nation* Day. There was no particular reason for this date other than the fact that our show would air on August 16—and it was Madonna's birthday, the day Elvis died, and the day the producer of this piece, Joanne Doroshow, was born. Other than that it had no special significance.

Bill took us over to Capitol Hill and past the security guards into the halls of Congress. As we strolled along the corridors of power, we shook a lot of hands and asked for support of our bill. We also handed out a number of gifts, which we thought would put the members of Congress in a better mood to consider our request.

We gave out free tube socks, pork rinds, key chains, Lady Remington electric shavers, Salad Shooters, and tickets to the Conan O'Brien show. It was heartwarming to see the delight on their faces when they received the free gifts. You got the feeling that every day was Christmas Day in the United States Congress.

But it wasn't until we walked into the office of Rep. Howard Coble, a conservative Republican from North Carolina, that we knew we had hit pay dirt. Coble was more than happy to see us. He is a kind, elderly gentleman who got our jokes about half the time. He loved the tube socks and the pork rinds. He wasn't quite sure what to do with a salad shooter, but he thanked us for it anyway.

When we gave him a "Thank You" card—inside of which we had slipped a $20 bill—he became upset. He politely refused it.

In the end, Bill convinced two congressmen to introduce the actual bill in Congress: Coble and Floyd Flake, a minister from New York City.

Then on May 10, 1994, during the 103rd Congress, in what must have been one of the most bizarre sights ever to occur on the floor of the U.S. House of Representatives, Coble and Flake read

Coble accepts the TV Nation gifts.

word for word the actual speeches we had written for them in support of *TV Nation* Day—and C-SPAN carried it live.

We were so excited, we didn't have time to wait for Congress to *pass* the law. After we aired the piece, we received hundreds of letters from fans wanting to celebrate *TV Nation* Day in their own communities. City councils, like the one in Orlando, Florida, passed resolutions declaring *TV Nation* Day in their community. The state legislature in Kansas passed three proclamations honoring *TV Nation*. The demand for *TV Nation* Day was sweeping the nation.

We decided that a day like this needed its own official, nationally televised parade, so the town of Fishkill, New York, offered to shut down for the day and celebrate the first-ever *TV Nation* Day on

---

Vol. 140   WASHINGTON, TUESDAY, MAY 10, 1994   No. 56

Congressional Record

INTRODUCTION OF A RESOLUTION DECLARING AUGUST 16, 1994, AS TV NATION DAY

(Mr. COBLE asked and was given permission to address the House for 1 minute and to revise and extend his remarks.)

Mr. COBLE. Mr. Speaker, many people often claim the media only shows what is wrong with America and not what is right about our great country. I am pleased to say that a new television program will air this summer that will be an uplifting, positive look at what is right about America.

The program will be known as TV Nation. It is a joint venture between NBC in the United States and the BBC in England. "TV Nation" will be different than most of the television magazine shows currently on the air. This show will be positive and upbeat and will not dwell on the negative aspects of today's society as so many of these tabloid journalism shows do.

I recently participated in an interview with Michael Moore, the host of the new show, and I am looking forward to seeing "TV Nation" later this summer. To support the program's goal of highlighting what is right about America and the world today, I am introducing a resolution declaring August 16, 1994, as "TV Nation Day."

The resolution, which I hope my colleagues will support, will praise "TV Nation" for creating new jobs in this country and improving our balance of trade, but more importantly, it will recognize the show's producers for allowing TV audiences in this country and around the world to see what is right about America, and that alone is a praiseworthy achievement.

August 16, 1994. The village municipal offices closed and gave their employees the day off. Other local businesses hung out "Closed for *TV Nation* Day" signs. They threw a big town party and held an incredible parade with marching bands, cheerleaders, a bicycle parade, floats and a walking television set.

The first baby born in Fishkill that morning was christened by our correspondent, Karen Duffy, as the first "*TV Nation* Baby." Spe-

cial ecumenical services were held for all the citizens of our blessed
TV Nation.

That night, thanks to the incredible skill and swiftness of the
TV Nation crew, the events in Fishkill were aired, some of them
live, on NBC. The network was a little more than nervous at letting
us go out over the airwaves with no prior censorship or approval
from the sponsors.

(In fact, one sponsor, McDonald's, pulled out ten minutes before
airtime because they did not have time to figure out which of their
seventeen prepared commercials should fit into the "tone" of the
show. There was something entertaining about watching the McDonald's guy running down the hall of NBC at 30 Rockefeller Center in
New York screaming about how we denied him the chance to place
his commercials. We spared the lives of many cows that night.)

It is an odd, eerie feeling, sitting in the master control room at
NBC, realizing that with a flick of a switch you determine what millions and millions of people are watching at that exact moment. It
was the only time we had seen the Mother Ship. In awe, we
reflected on the day and our good fortune. Why had they let us in
the control room? Why were *we* on TV?

Fishkill residents proudly march with their television sets.

These were questions to be pondered at some other time because, right then, the guy from McDonald's had accidentally locked himself in a men's room stall.

First things first. Happy *TV Nation* Day, America!

103D CONGRESS
2D SESSION **H. J. RES. 365**

To designate August 16, 1994, as "TV Nation Day".

IN THE HOUSE OF REPRESENTATIVES

MAY 10, 1994

Mr. COBLE (for himself and Mr. FLAKE) introduced the following joint resolution; which was referred to the Committee on Post Office and Civil Service

---

JOINT RESOLUTION

To designate August 16, 1994, as "TV Nation Day".

Whereas television is one industry with which no other country can compete with America;

Whereas American popular culture is a major United States export;

Whereas some of the most memorable and uplifting moments in people's lives have occurred while watching television, from the Apollo moon landing to little baby Jessica's rescue from the well;

Whereas TV Nation will air on broadcast television in the United States, making it available, free of charge, to everyone;

Whereas TV Nation is the first American/European joint television venture, and will begin a new opportunity for similar ventures in the future;

Whereas other news magazine programs focus on what's wrong with America, TV Nation focuses on what's right;

Whereas TV Nation will help the United States economy by providing many new employment opportunities, particularly high-tech information ones; and

Whereas TV Nation employs numerous Oscar, Emmy, and Cable-Ace Award nominees and winners: Now, therefore, be it

1   *Resolved*, That August 16, 1994, shall be designated
2 as "TV Nation Day".

○

25

Whiny White Guys

For over two centuries, the United States of America had a strong, aggressive affirmative action policy. Since the days of the Founding Fathers, the leaders of our government, our businesses, and our educational institutions have firmly believed that quotas and preferential hiring were the cornerstone of our system.

As long as those getting the preferential treatment were the white guys.

In the 1970s, laws were enacted to help equalize an unequal situation. Women and minorities were given a leg up on the system, and colleges and businesses were encouraged to look harder and find qualified blacks, Hispanics, and females who, in the past, were overlooked because they had no connection to the program.

Connection was what the old affirmative action arrangement was all about. Dad went to Princeton because Granddad went to Princeton and now Sonny will go to Princeton because the university gives preference to the offspring of alumni. Or Fred at the bank knows So-and-So is good for the loan because Fred and So-and-So both belong to the Rotary. So-and-So is thus a beneficiary of affirmative action.

Women were not even allowed to vote until the 1920s. African Americans to this day still live with the effects of their great-great-grandparents having been slaves—and their social condition has remained virtually unchanged in over 130 years of "freedom." The system of privilege and power is passed on from one generation to the next, with each ensuring that the way things are will stay unchanged. If you don't have power to begin with, you're out of luck.

Some people thought a new form of affirmative action was needed. Those in power have successfully resisted this and stopped it in its tracks. These days, the concept of making one's institution "all-inclusive" seems as dated as bell-bottoms.

Why are white guys so afraid of sharing power? What is it about women and blacks that makes them quiver with fear? Don't they know how ridiculous they look whining about how "those people" are taking all the good jobs?

Look at those sniveling little brats at the Virginia Military Academy and you see how pathetic this is. They didn't want girls admitted to The Citadel. They fought it in court and they lost. When the girls were finally allowed, they treated them so harshly that the first two quit. Why were they so afraid of this integration? Did girls frighten them? Were they scared that the girls might be smarter or, God forbid, stronger? How would they ever recover from that kind of humiliation?

Our question is: Are these the kind of men we want in our military defending our country? What's going to happen when they have to face a real enemy?

Frankly, we find this all real embarrassing. Our country's filled with whiny white men who are afraid to compete with minorities for jobs, education, or power. The old affirmative action system made sure that women and blacks never entered the game. When blacks were finally allowed to enter sports (one of the first experiments of New Affirmative Action), they kicked our ass. Whoa! What if they—and women—did the same in the office or in the classroom?

We think that's why the white guys are whining about how they are now the "new minority"—that it's the white man who has the hardest time finding a job because even though he is the "most qualified," he has been passed over for a woman or an African American. This is the common pout of the white man in America, and there's nothing more silly looking than a grown man pouting—especially when only 9 percent of the Senate is made up of women, blacks represent just over 5 percent of all journalists, and there are no African Americans on the board of directors of many of our largest companies.

At *TV Nation,* we decided to write an ode to the Whiny White Guy. Done in the style of one of those bleak documentaries on PBS that warn of the extinction of entire species of insects, we issued our dire plea to the people of America to save the white man at all costs. Protect him and his habitat before it is too late!

A PUBLIC SERVICE ANNOUNCEMENT

by Jay Martel

The White Man.

He's everywhere.

Great white men include leaders, entrepreneurs, and artists.

For centuries the White Man has expanded his habitat to every corner of the earth. He's invented everything from the A-bomb to the Zamboni. Surely this sparkling example of the human species will be with us forever, or will he?

Maybe, like the mighty buffalo, we have taken the White Man for granted. Already there are disturbing signs that the White Man as we know him is an endangered species.

The attack has taken its toll, everywhere you look the White Man is in decline. Ten years ago, 96 percent of the U.S. Senate was composed of white males. Today that figure has dwindled to a scant 89 percent! In the last few years the corporate boardrooms, the traditional habitat of white men, has undergone an unprecedented invasion by outsiders. Today the number of white males has plunged to merely 30 percent more than everyone else. Truly the White Male is being threatened on all sides by his natural enemies. Women. Minorities. And basically everyone who isn't a white male. He's fighting back the only way he knows how.

TV Nation writer Jay Martel reviews ideas with Michael Moore.

But he's tired and who knows how long he'll hold up without our help. While environmentalists demonstrate on behalf of the spotted owl and the snail darter there has been some reluctance to help the White Man.

Yet without the White Man we are all worse off. Who will bring us the A-bomb and Zambonis of tomorrow? Who will paint their faces at football games?

The White Man clearly needs our help. Support *TV Nation*'s efforts to get the White Man recognized as an endangered species by sending your letters to the U.S. Fish and Wildlife Service. Remember: a White Man is a terrible thing to waste.

26

The Censored
TV Nation

As you may have noticed throughout this book, getting the networks to carry much of what we do is no easy task. On one level, we are the antithesis of everything their corporate owners stand for. We believe a diversity of voices in the media strengthens the democracy. The corporations believe in eliminating diversity and having only a few companies control the media and the "news" it presents to the public. We believe that the real power in America rests with the moneyed interests, and that the 1 percent who control 50 percent of the country's wealth should be challenged every step of the way. They believe that the media should celebrate this wealth, that its critics should be silent, and that every seven minutes a brand of beer or tortilla chips should be hawked to the unsuspecting consumer. We believe that humor is a powerful tool in illuminating the issues we care about. They think we're funny—and, mostly, harmless.

Because the bottom line and the desire for maximum profit reigns supreme at the networks, as long as *TV Nation* sold its expected allotment of Doritos and Budweiser, we were allowed to do our show pretty much the way we wanted.

So when people ask us, "How in the heck did you get that on the air?" our answer is, "Networks are not like us. They do not have 'feelings' or 'politics.' There is a bottom line. And our bottom line, within their desired demographics, was very, very good."

Of course, there are exceptions to every rule, including this one. We did things on *TV Nation* that went beyond what the networks could take. When that happened, the strong arm of the censor came crashing down on us, and it was without pity or concern for our blathering about First Amendment rights.

Of the 105 segments we shot for *TV Nation*, only 5 were banned by the American networks. (Those five all ran on the BBC and in twenty foreign countries).

The season on NBC was actually the easiest for us. We got through the entire summer without a single story being censored. Those included our visit to the Mexican office of NBC's corporate parent, GE, and our attempts to buy congressmen.

In December, NBC asked us to do a year-end special. We jumped at the chance. Included in the show were the segments featuring the Corp-Aid concert for Exxon, hiring a rent-a-cop for Clinton, and picking a new enemy for the United States (France won).

But the main segment in the year-end special was a scary look at the subculture within the anti-abortion movement that believes it is acceptable to threaten doctors who perform abortions. Our correspondent, Louis Theroux, spent a weekend with an anti-abortion activist, Roy MacMillan, in Jackson, Mississippi. Roy took Louis to the abortion clinic where he harasses women as they walk in the door. Roy explained that he felt it was morally correct to do whatever is necessary to defend the "rights of the unborn." When Louis asked, "Do you think it would be justifiable homicide to execute the president?" Roy replied, "I think he's probably in harm's way by acknowledging and endorsing the killing. . . . It would probably to me be more justifiable to, uh, assassinate the Supreme Court judges."

Are those comments are a violation of the law? It is a felony to issue a real or implied threat against the president of the United States. We thought that the Secret Service might arrest Roy MacMillan once they saw the show.

Early on in production NBC gave the go-ahead, even though the network was concerned with the controversial nature of the story. But, just days before the year-end special was to air, the network called to say that all the sponsors had pulled out. None of them wanted any of their ads next to a segment dealing with abortion. NBC tried to find advertisers who would be willing to take the risk, but there were none. It was the week before Christmas, and we found it impossible to save the segment. NBC told us that they could not air a show without commercials (though to their credit they had courageously done so with a TV movie a few years back called *Roe v. Wade*). We relented, and the segment was pulled from the show.

Louis Theroux looks on as Roy MacMillan yells at women entering the clinic.

Two days after the special aired, a young man named John Salvi III, who considered himself part of the extreme end of the anti-abortion movement, went into two clinics in Brookline, Massachusetts, and shot four clinic workers, killing two of them.

Would this man have been as brazen if he had seen a spokesman of his cause being taken away in handcuffs on television the night before? That is the effect one hopes for in arresting a criminal—to dissuade others from committing crimes.

The Secret Service called and demanded a copy of our censored segment. We are not in the business of gathering evidence for the police and did not provide the segment to them. If we didn't have a broadcasting system where advertisers have the power to get a piece killed, the Secret Service would already have their own copy, compliments of the VCR.

The special did air uncensored in the U.K., so the Feds contacted the BBC, who seemed more than happy to assist the American government.

The Savings and Loan Scandal

Did you ever wonder what happened to all those men who ran the savings and loan institutions in the 1980s? Their negligent, often criminal behavior resulted in their customers—and the taxpayers—losing billions of dollars.

We wanted to know: Did they ever go to jail? Did they have to make reparations?

What we discovered is that the majority served *no* prison time and, in fact, have prospered long after their clients went bankrupt. They even formed a support group to help each other cope with the public's negative reaction toward them.

Pam Yates, a *TV Nation* producer, convinced these men and women to let us film their support group meeting and to hang out with them at their new jobs. Many are millionaires again.

This segment was an incredible piece of television; if you weren't laughing, you wanted to punch your TV. There was only one problem. The American public never got to see the segment. For some unexplained reason, Fox told us it could not air. Their only attempted explanation was that the S&L scandal was "old news" and that our mentions of former presidents Reagan and Bush would not interest their "young adult and teen demographic."

We wondered if the S&L executives we filmed had second thoughts and called the Fox Network to put a stop to the segment.

Columbia TriStar, which has committed to placing all the censored segments on various volumes of the *TV Nation* home video, has informed us that this is the one censored segment that will not be placed on the videos.

Gay Bashing in Topeka

As described in Michael's book, *Downsize This!*, there is a high school in Topeka, Kansas, that gave extra credit to a student who picketed the funerals of people who had died of AIDS, holding a sign that read "GOD HATES FAGS." We sent our crew to Topeka

Picking up a little extra credit after school.

to do a story on this student and his family. The entire clan demonstrates and pickets anyone they suspect of being homosexual. It was both weird and frightening.

The Fox Network told us that gay issues scare advertisers away. They allowed us to do one "gay story" (our Love Night serenade to Jesse Helms) and then drew the line.

Small Condoms

Until a few years ago, condoms always came in one size—regular, or "one size fits all."

Then, suddenly, there appeared a new size of condom on the pharmacy shelves—EXTRA LARGE. MAGNUM. MAX. Leave it to a product designed by and for men that they would come in only these two sizes—regular and EXTRA LARGE. MAGNUM. MAX.

But what about that other all-important size—*small*? Why are there no small-size condoms?

We sent our guest reporter and old friend from Flint, Ben Hamper (author of *Rivethead*), to various drugstores around New York to ask them if they had any small-size condoms.

The responses Ben got included shock, hysterics, disbelief, and confusion. After seeing the footage we were convinced that this was an entertaining way to talk about condoms.

NBC and Fox did not see it that way. When we showed the finished segment to the suits at NBC, one of them told us that "if we air this we'll lose affiliates in the South."

"Why the South?" we asked.

"Because you cannot conjure up the image of a small penis on network television for a full seven minutes and expect people in the South to watch it!"

"But," Michael protested, "they're airing it on the BBC in England!"

"Exactly my point!"

Now, that was some logic.

We were also told that because our show aired in the "family hour," we would not be allowed to say the word *condom* so many times.

We felt that talking about condoms *should* happen in the "family hour." Both networks disagreed.

Meanwhile, one out of every hundred people on this planet is infected with HIV.

Reenacting the L.A. Riots

Have you ever been to a Fourth of July celebration and watched a group of grown men reenact Civil War battles in full period costume? Everyone seems to have a good time rooting for the Blue or the Gray and cheering the spectacle.

Maybe the reason this all seems like fun is that the Civil War was a long time ago and none of us know any of the six hundred thousand people who lost their lives. But would all of this be just as entertaining if it were a bunch of guys reenacting a more recent war?

We asked a group of Civil War reenactors if they would, in full uniform, engage in battles that occurred not so long ago. They agreed, and before a group of happy picnickers, they reenacted the dropping of The Bomb on Hiroshima. (We rented a World War II bomber and flew it over the soldiers—and they all dropped dead.) We then asked them to reenact the bombing of Nagasaki. Same thing. After that they reenacted the fall of Saigon.

The Fox Network hated this. But after much wrangling, and a promise by Michael to make it clear in his narrated introduction that he, too, thought this was sick, they agreed to air three sections of it.

But they refused to include the final piece of War Reenactment Night—the Civil War "veterans" staging the Los Angeles riots. We shot it in three parts—the beating of Rodney King, the Simi Valley jury finding the police not guilty, and the ensuing uprising.

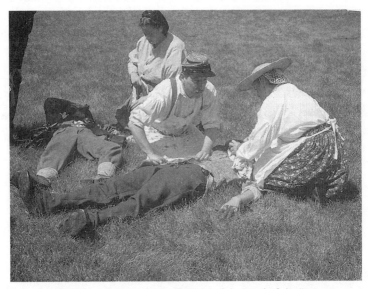

Civil War reenactors assist the injured during the L.A. riots.

This simulation made the network executives very uneasy. Of course, they all live in Los Angeles. Satirizing the slaughter of a couple hundred thousand Japanese was passable, but to take on the racial situation in Los Angeles . . . whoa! Turn off the television!

This section of our war reenactment segment did not air.

For the most part, we found that when we stood our ground and insisted that our stories run intact, they did. Perhaps all too often in Hollywood, producers cave in when they don't need to. It's not that they are afraid of the network brass, it's just that the suits can wear you down, and giving in is the easiest thing to do.

The most important thing we learned is that everything you see on network television has already been seen and approved by some advertiser who is buying time on that show. They actually view and approve (or censor) the shows before they air.

We also learned that the reasons for television censorship are not just sex and violence and language. Sometimes, *ideas* are just too dangerous to air.

27

When All Is Said and Done

On September 8, 1995, the last episode of *TV Nation* aired. The following night, at the 47th Annual Primetime Emmy Awards at the Shrine Auditorium in Los Angeles, *TV Nation* won the Emmy award for Outstanding Informational Series. In accepting our statue, we thanked "General Motors, General Electric, and General Murdoch—without them, we wouldn't be here."

There is a popular misconception that *TV Nation* was canceled. That was never the case. The show was only ordered for eight episodes each year as a summer replacement series. It took us eight months of work to produce just eight shows, so it would have been pretty tough to have been on weekly throughout the year and maintain any level of quality.

TV Nation senior producer David Wald, executive producer Michael Moore, producer Kathleen Glynn, and supervising producer Jerry Kupfer.

Despite the unprecedented amount of fan mail they received, both NBC and Fox decided against ordering any future episodes of *TV Nation*. However, they did meet with us to consider other projects. In November 1997 we shot a pilot for a late-night show for Fox. It contained *TV Nation*-type segments (Mike tries to give Bill Gates a housewarming gift, we try to find Joe Camel a new job) and interviews with Sheryl Crow, Jon Stewart, director Kevin Smith, and O. J. Simpson.

That's right.

O. J.

It was the first time he faced a live audience in the three and a half years since the murder of his ex-wife. It was a riveting hour, and as this book goes to press, it's anyone's guess if this show will ever be seen by the public.

In March of 1998, we received some good news. Channel Four Television, one of Great Britain's major television networks, agreed to finance sixteen episodes of a new comedy-reality show similar to

TV Nation. Michael Jackson, the former head of BBC 1 and 2 and our original champion, took the job as the new head of Channel Four and immediately offered to bring back our show. So we said yes. He has also agreed to produce a new late-night talk show, an independent film series that Michael will host, and our next two feature films, one fiction, the other documentary. It is, to say the least, a welcome show of support. Channel Four is currently negotiating deals for these programs to air on American networks. Kind of a cool reverse-foreign-aid package.

How do we feel about our experience of working on *TV Nation*? In the battle between art and commerce, commerce virtually always wins. For two summers we were able to dodge most of the bullets and come out with our sense of humor and conscience intact.

We wonder, as we look back, why more of television doesn't aspire to something better than shows that reinforce stereotypes, won't question the status quo, or appeal to the severely brain dead. Don't the executives read their own ratings sheets? The top ten shows in any given week are productions like *ER, Seinfeld, 60 Minutes, The Simpsons, Frasier*—the smarter shows. People don't want to watch dumb TV. Hollywood should take that cue and start producing more risky, subversive television.

TV Nation did no better or worse in its time slot than the other shows that had occupied its spot in the past or since we went off the air. And while we never made it into the top forty, we did a lot better than *Cheers, M*A*S*H,* or *Seinfeld* did in their first years—all shows that ended their initial runs at the bottom of the ratings heap.

We closed our last show with the first idea Mike pitched the executives at NBC in that original meeting back in 1993: "The Consumers Guide to Confession." Because Mike believes there is a better chance than not that we will all have to face St. Peter at the Pearly Gates one day, he chickened out on confessing his sin in twenty different churches. Instead, he asked fellow recovering Catholic Janeane Garofalo to perform the experiment. She was convinced that she was already doomed for Hades, so she enthusiastically agreed to go to Confession.

She confessed her sins, lightning didn't strike her dead, and Janeane went on to become a star. The ratings for that show were among our highest. The staff, as it had on the sixteen previous show nights, got together to watch the show and party into the night. We had our usual laugh when we saw who was sponsoring that evening's show (AT&T, Coca-Cola, Burger King, and Sara Lee) and we toasted each other for surviving all the hard work.

That night, we all felt that this may have been the best work we had ever done, and we wondered if it would make a difference. To us, it wasn't just a TV show. It was a video Molotov we threw into a medium we hoped to shake up a bit. Did it work? It did if you feel like putting down this book and going out and raising a little hell yourself.

Appendix A

The *TV Nation* Polls

The following are actual opinion polls of the American public conducted by the polling firm of Widgery and Associates. There is a margin of error of plus or minus 9%.

NBC Show 1

65% of all Americans believe that frozen pizza will never be any good and there's nothing science can do about it.

10% of the American public would pay $5 to see Senator Orrin Hatch (R-Utah) fight a big mean dog on Pay TV.
86% of all viewers would root for the dog.
100% of women viewers would root for the dog.

45% of Americans think rain doesn't feel as good in real life as it seems to in the movies.

16% of Perot voters believe "If dolphins were really smart, they could get out of those nets."

NBC Show 2

65% of American women believe there is "a lot of difference" between a campaign contribution and a bribe.
Only 35% of men see a difference.

70% of American women have never had an emotionally satisfying relationship with a Republican.

NBC Show 3

In the past year 36% of Americans have chanted "We're Number One!" Only 22% of Bush voters have chanted "We're Number One!"

62% of Americans believe that a trip to a major theme park is more culturally enriching than a trip to the Reagan Library.

NBC Show 4

39% of Americans believe that guns are not "as dangerous as they say."

15% of Americans wish Dennis Hopper would go back on drugs.

NBC Show 5

29% of Americans believe that Elvis was right to shoot TV sets.

29% of Perot voters say, "The candidate I vote for usually loses."

NBC Show 6

11% of Americans who suffer from indigestion would rather retake the SAT than watch a Jesse Helms filibuster.

12.5% of Americans who voted for Clinton believe that they will someday be told "just what Victoria's Secret is."

98% of Bush voters believe they will never know.

NBC Show 7

88% of Bush voters "have no idea what rappers are talking about."

14% of Americans surveyed agree that Puerto Rico should not be the fifty-first state because "that extra star would make the flag look bad."

NBC Year-End Special (1994)

35% of Americans believe Richard Nixon went to heaven.
59% believe he went "somewhere else."

34% of those who voted in the last election believe *Forrest Gump* was a documentary.

Fox Show 1

60% of Americans say that if they could push a button that would make Larry King disappear, they would "keep pushing it and not stop."

37% of Americans agree that while they would hate being British, they wouldn't mind having a British accent.

More Americans say they would rather spend time in a Jacuzzi with Dan Rather than with Tom Brokaw.
Of those who would tub with Dan, 10% have no health insurance.

Fox Show 2

11% of people who have tried Prozac would like to see Dan Quayle make a comeback because "Al Gore just isn't funny enough."

36% of college graduates think that there are virtually no female serial killers because women "just aren't aggressive enough."

Fox Show 3

12% of those polled believe the success of actor David Hasselhoff, star of *Baywatch,* is due at least in part to "dealings with the devil."

45% of Americans believe that if space aliens could pick up C-SPAN and see Sonny Bono speaking on the floor of Congress, they would never visit the Earth.

17% of college graduates would punch themselves really hard in the face for $50.

28% of those who said they were "normal" Americans would like to be king of Great Britain, but not if it meant marrying the queen.

Fox Show 4

44% of Republicans said they would watch *Nightline* if it had a band and an opening comedy monologue.

If Jesus came back and saw that Pat Robertson was his spokesperson, 46% of Americans think that we'd all be in big trouble.

42% of Americans feel that Kato Kaelin should be a passenger on the next space shuttle, whether he wants to go or not.

Fox Show 5

26% of those in possession of a firearm believe that the Second Amendment protects their right to buy explosive fertilizer.

81% of those who have seen two or more *Police Academy* movies believe that O. J. is innocent.

29% of those surveyed think that the guy who first put the "Great" in front of "Britain" probably meant it as a joke.

Fox Show 6

16% of all Americans believe that the world is out to get them. Of those, 46% are gun owners.

One-third of American women agree that baseball was more exciting when it was on strike.

40% of Americans remember where they were when *JFK* the movie was shot.

Fox Show 7

Of those who said they've had a good cry in the past six months, 42% were Democrats, 27% were Republicans, and 54% said they believe in UFOs.

28% of Americans think that our army's high-tech military equipment is too expensive to risk in combat.

Appendix B

The Shows

We shot 105 segments for *TV Nation*. Here is a rundown of every American broadcast.

NBC Show 1
Original airdate: July 19, 1994.

NAFTA
TV Nation travels to Mexico to take advantage of the North American Free Trade Agreement by hiring Mexicans at eighty cents an hour to produce the show.

TAXI (See page 74)

APPLETON
Appleton, Minnesota, has hit hard times lately. A prison is built to help boost the economy—the only thing missing is inmates. We find out why.

LOVE CANAL
Remember the toxic Love Canal near Niagara Falls? Industrious Realtors are trying to convince people to move back to the new less-toxic community.

MIKE'S MISSILE (See page 125)

NBC Show 2
Original airdate: July 26, 1994.

THE CEO CHALLENGE (See page 60)

AIDS INSURANCE BROKERS
We investigate brokers who make available to investors the life insurance policies of AIDS patients at discount prices. When the patient dies, investors claim the entire value of the policy and make a huge profit.

KLAN PR MAKEOVER
TV Nation meets the "National Director" of the new, media-savvy Ku Klux Klan to see how the Klan's rhetoric is made more appealing.

KUWAIT
Remember the Gulf War when Allied troops went to Kuwait to defeat the Iraqis and restore democracy? *TV Nation* travels to liberated, democratic Kuwait to find out if the Gulf War really did bring democracy to a country where, for example, women cannot vote.

PETS ON PROZAC
TV Nation checks up on a number of pets that have been prescribed Prozac by their veterinarians to see if the drug has helped.

Karen Duffy freezes in Fargo.

Correspondent Roy Sekoff proudly rides the sludge train.

NBC Show 3

Original airdate: August 2, 1994.

A DAY WITH DR. DEATH (See page 86)

WE HIRE OUR OWN LOBBYIST (See page 179)

AMAZON AVON

TV Nation travels to the Amazon to visit Avon representatives who sell cosmetics to women who live deep in the rain forest. The Avon products can cost up to thirteen times their daily wage.

NORTH DAKOTA

North Dakota is the least visited state in the United States. *TV Nation* investigates attractions like the Lawrence Welk Museum and the geographical center of North America in subzero temperatures.

SLUDGE

What happens after New Yorkers flush the toilet? *TV Nation* follows the sludge train all the way to Sierra Blanca, Texas, where New York's sludge is shipped and spread around town.

NBC Show 4

Original airdate: August 9, 1994.

O. J./PRODUCT PLACEMENT NIGHT

TV Nation jumps on the free advertising bandwagon and visits O. J.'s Bronco dealer to learn about the "O. J. Special." We also offer free advertising by strategically placing various products throughout the show.

1–800–TOURISM

We visit a prison where inmates are being used by the state tourist department as a source of cheap labor.

HOT SPRINGS

TV Nation travels to the town where President Clinton grew up, a strange resort town in Arkansas called Hot Springs.

LORD MIKE

Lord of the Manor of FOLESHILL Coventry, England

"No Lord Does It Like This Lord"
This card good for one free drink

LORD MIKE

What does it take to become royalty? Family connections? *TV Nation* visits Britain to learn what it really takes— about $8,000. And they take the Diners Club card!

HEALTH CARE OLYMPICS (See page 154)

NBC Show 5

Original airdate: August 16, 1994.

TV NATION DAY (See page 179)

MILLENNIUM

There are over 2,500 groups in the United States who feel the end of the world as we know it will come with the new millennium. *TV Nation* visits four of these groups to find out if we will survive the year 2000.

ARE YOU PREPARED FOR PRISON? (See page 91)

HAULIN' COMMUNISM (See page 134)

MAKING PEACE WITH PIZZA (See page 173)

NBC Fifth Anniversary Special
Original airdate: August 21, 1994.

Compilation broadcast of first five shows.

NBC Show 6
Original airdate: August 23, 1994.

GUN NIGHT
TV Nation correspondents join the ranks of actor Christian Slater, crooner Harry Connick, Jr., Dallas Cowboys coach Barry Switzer, and congressmen's wives—and pack heat! We exercise our right not only to bear arms, but to shoot them too!

WITH NEIGHBORS LIKE THESE (See page 149)

NY/NJ GREASE
TV Nation uses its leverage to get tax breaks for running its operation in New York City by threatening to move to New Jersey. We go right to the top—New York City mayor Rudolph Giuliani—to see what we can get.

TALK SHOW
TV Nation attempts to answer the commonly asked question: Where exactly do those people on daytime talk shows come from?

NBC Show 7
Original airdate: August 30, 1994.

GOLF NIGHT
TV Nation elicits the help of Michigan golf pro Rodger Jabara for hints on how to improve the show—and that terrible slice.

Caning

What was the British Empire built on? According to some British people—caning. *TV Nation* risks its butt and visits Great Britain to get the story.

Sabotage (See page 111)

Junk Mail (See page 101)

Corporate Consultants

Many companies actually hire consultants to help them downsize more effectively, so we decided to hire our own consultant to trim the fat on our payroll.

NBC Year-End Special (1994)

Original airdate: December 28, 1994.

Jacuzzi

Throughout the show *TV Nation* gives Jacuzzi limousine rides to members of the most hated groups in America including landlords, telemarketers, and satanists.

The Corp-Aid Concert (See page 39)

White House Security Guard

The White House seems to have been under assault lately—a man flies his plane into it, a man shoots at it. *TV Nation* hires a private security guard for the most important address in the free world.

Didn't Die in '94

End-of-the-year television specials always talk about the people that died in the previous year. We at *TV Nation* think that is depressing so throughout the night we highlight the people who did not die in 1994.

'95 Invasion

The past few years have been busy ones for American troops: trips to Haiti, Somalia, and Kuwait. *TV Nation* holds a vote for the American public to decide where the troops will invade in 1995.

Meet the Republicans

TV Nation takes a look at careers and rhetoric of the men and . . . the men that have been elected in overwhelming numbers to run our country—the Republicans!

New Year Predictions

Steven Wright consults a number of experts on the major events that will or will not occur in 1995.

New Jobs

TV Nation talks to a number of people in Scranton, Pennsylvania, to see what "new" jobs they have gotten and how their lives have improved since the creation of these jobs during the Clinton administration.

Fox Show 1

Original airdate: July 28, 1995.

Bruno for President

With such easy qualifications for becoming President—a candidate must be a thirty-five-year-old native-born citizen—why do we always have so few choices? *TV Nation* runs its own

candidate, convicted felon Louie Bruno, to take part in the democratic process.

WE'RE #1

TV Nation visits cities in America in celebration of their status as #1 in various fields such as *Playboy* subscriptions (Des Moines, Iowa) and carjacking (Tampa, Florida).

INVADING THE BEACH AT GREENWICH, CONNECTICUT (See page 22)

CRIME SCENE CLEANUP

TV Nation meets the Barneses, a couple who started a business to cash in on the rise in violent crimes by cleaning up crime scenes. After the bodies are cleared and the police have gone, the Barneses move in, do their business, and collect a hefty profit.

SLAVES (See page 81)

CRACKERS, THE CORPORATE CRIME-FIGHTING CHICKEN (See page 46)

Fox Show 2
Original airdate: August 4, 1995.

PAYBACK TIME (See page 30)

KGB—YURI, OUR *TV NATION* SPY (See page 117)

NEA

Many members of Congress want to eliminate funding for the National Endowment for the Arts and let private enterprise pay for our artists and museums. *TV Nation* says, "Hey, not a bad idea!" and tours those museums that currently thrive without a single penny from the NEA—the Kentucky Fried Chicken Museum, the Tobacco Art and History Museum, and the Sacred Arts Museum.

A-BOMB

TV Nation visits an Idaho man who bought 750 tons of scrap metal at a government auction. To his surprise, when he got the scrap metal home it turned out to be the makings of an atomic bomb factory.

JERUSALEM SYNDROME

Occasionally, a few of the millions of tourists who visit the Holy Land get off the tour bus and believe they are Jesus. Doctors in Jerusalem have named this phenomenon the "Jerusalem Syndrome." *TV Nation* walks the path of the prophets to investigate.

THE JOHNS OF JUSTICE (See page 142)

Fox Show 3

Original airdate: August 11, 1995.

WAR REENACTMENT NIGHT

TV Nation joins the guys who dress up on weekends and reenact Civil War battles. Only this time, we have them reenact more recent battles in full Civil War regalia—the fall of Saigon, the Battle of Hiroshima, and the battle between Tom Arnold and Roseanne.

HELLTOWN

The Southern Baptist Church has published a map in Alabama showing which counties have the most residents who are "unsaved" and therefore doomed to the fires of hell. *TV Nation* travels to the county with the most "lost" souls and attempts to save them from eternal damnation.

CRACKERS TOUR—PHILADELPHIA (See page 52)

ELECTRONIC SNIFFER

Just when you thought machines had replaced everyone—now comes the electronic nose. Around the world thousands of people are employed by companies to test the smell of new products, whether pleasant or not. *TV Nation* visits two companies in Great Britain that want to replace human sniffers with electronic ones.

COBB COUNTY (See page 163)

SCHOOL OF THE AMERICAS

The United States has established a school in Georgia to train Latin American soldiers in the art of "population control." It's called School of the Americas. A number of Latin American "strongmen"

(Manuel Noriega, for example) have received their education there—compliments of the American taxpayer.

WIDGERY
Did you ever wonder if the polls that appear on *TV Nation* are real? Many viewers do. So we introduce our viewers to Widgery and Associates, the legitimate polling firm that polls for *TV Nation*.

Fox Show 4
Original airdate: August 18, 1995.

BRIAN ANTHONY HARRIS IS NOT WANTED (See page 69)

LOVE NIGHT (See page 14)

AQUARIUM
Places like Camden, New Jersey, Long Beach, California, and Tulsa, Oklahoma, struggling to get by, have turned to big fish tanks to boost tourism and hopefully save their inner cities. *TV Nation* investigates.

MIKE'S MILITIA
Since the Oklahoma City bombing much attention has been paid to the Michigan Militia, an armed group of disgruntled citizens whom Timothy McVeigh and the Nichols brothers consorted with in 1993. *TV Nation* spends a day with the Militia and attempts to get them to put down their guns, to take off their camouflage, and to encourage them to participate in the democratic process.

KGB—THE COMPETITION (See page 123)

Fox Show 5
Original airdate: August 25, 1995.

CANADA NIGHT
TV Nation's special salute to our neighbors to the north. Throughout the night we smuggle illegal Canadians across the border, try to give free guns to Canadians, and attempt to find out how much Americans know about Canada.

D.C. PERKS

The Contract with America states that Congress must abide by all the laws that the citizens of the United States do. As it turns out, Congress still plays and lives by a different set of rules. *TV Nation* travels to Washington, D.C., to enforce the Contract with America by showing up and asking for the same treatment members of Congress receive.

NUGENT

TV Nation visits the newest board member of the National Rifle Association, rock 'n' roll legend Ted Nugent. Ted gives our correspondent, Louis Theroux, a tour of his Michigan farm and expounds on various issues from assault weapons to Janet Reno and confirms his newfound status as the "Rock 'n' Roll Rush Limbaugh."

CRACKERS TOUR — ST. LOUIS (See page 54)

I WANT TO BE AN ARGENTINEAN (See page 95)

Fox Show 6
Original airdate: September 1, 1995.

HUG-A-GOV

The new Congress has said it wants to return more power to the states. If that's where the power is, we at *TV Nation* want to reach out and touch that power. Thus begins Michael Moore's mission: to hug all fifty governors.

PSY-OPS

Coverage of the O.J. Simpson trial was important, but did it require three hundred reporters a day? Were there not other serious stories to cover? *TV Nation* hired its own psychological operations expert, retired from the U.S. Army, to help conduct a "psy-op" program to destabilize and reduce the massive amount of O.J. coverage.

ROSEMONT

Sections of Rosemont, Illinois, an affluent Chicago suburb, are closed off to the outside world, and the area has even placed police guard booths on public streets leading into their city—so that only residents are allowed in. *TV Nation* goes to the outskirts of Rosemont to set up its own guard booth and prevent citizens of Rosemont from entering Chicago.

UNIONS

Everyone knows unions are dying or dead. But there are whole new groups of employees out there that are starting to unionize for the first time: the Buffalo Bills cheerleading squad; the topless dancers at a bar in New Jersey; the cartoon characters at Disney World. *TV Nation* says, "Show us your union label!"

WHINY WHITE GUYS (See page 187)

BRIAN ANTHONY HARRIS IS NOT WANTED, PART 2 (See page 69)

FAN MAIL

TV Nation's own candidate for president, Louie Bruno, and his campaign manager, Lucky, answer our viewer mail.

Louie Bruno and Lucky Dellacaprini read the mail.

Fox Show 7

Original airdate: September 8, 1995.

BULLY REUNION NIGHT

Each *TV Nation* correspondent is reunited with his or her bully from high school. The bullies are flown to New York for a special fun-filled weekend of carriage rides through Central Park, tandem bicycle rides, and a little payback.

CONFESSION

Once a year all Catholics are required to go to Confession to confess their annual sins. Interestingly enough, no two priests give the same penance for the same sins. As a service to our Catholic viewers, *TV Nation* presents the first ever "Consumer's Guide to the Confessional."

TV FELONS

TV Nation travels through Britain with the "TV Cops" as they bust British citizens who have plugged in their television sets without a license from the British government.

CRACKERS TOUR—DETROIT (See page 55)

KGB—DEMOCRATIC PARTY (See page 122)

WEATHERMAN
TV Nation hires a weatherman who was fired for refusing to lie and
forecasting rain on the day of a big Republican picnic.

Censored Segments

GAY BASHING IN TOPEKA (See page 195)

S&L (See page 194)

ABORTION (See page 192)

SMALL CONDOMS (See page 196)

WAR REENACTMENT NIGHT—THE L.A. RIOTS (See page 197)

*New York Mayor Rudloph Giuliani presents
Mike with his Emmy nomination
just weeks after the visit from Crackers.*

Appendix C

How to Get Stuff

We often get calls and letters from people who would like information on how to get our books and videotapes. Here's the scoop.

Roger & Me, TV Nation Vols. 1 & 2, and *Canadian Bacon*

Available on home video from Critic's Choice, list price: $14.95 for each tape plus shipping and handling.

To order call: 800–367–7765

(Please note: *Pets or Meat, The Return to Flint* (1992) will be available in the future.)

Downsize This! Random Threats from an Unarmed American by Michael Moore

Available at your local bookshop or by post from:

Book Service by Post

PO Box 29, Douglas, Isle of Man, IM99 1BQ

Credit cards accepted. For details: Telephone: 01624 675137,

Fax: 01624 670923

Email: bookshop@enterprise.net

Free post and packing in the UK.

Overseas customers: add £1 per book (paperback) and £3 per book (hardback).

The Big One

Available October 1998 from Buena Vista Home Video or at your local video store.

Appendix D

TV Nation Resources

The following are addresses, telephone numbers, and Websites of interest. Take action and use these as needed.

Who Let This Show on the Air?

TriStar Television
10202 West Washington Blvd.
Culver City, CA 90232
310–244–4000
www.spe.sony.com/tv

BBC Television
Viewer and Listener
    Correspondence
The Broadway
Ealing
London W5 2PA
ENGLAND
0181 743 8000
www.bbc.co.uk

Channel Four Television
124 Horseferry Road
London SW1P 2TX
ENGLAND
0171 306 8333
www.channel4.com

NBC Television
30 Rockefeller Plaza
New York, NY 10112
212–664–4444
www.nbc.com

Fox Television
PO Box 900
Beverly Hills, CA 90213
310–395–2294
www.foxnetwork.com

Love Night

Anti-Defamation League
823 UN Plaza
New York, NY 10017
212–885–7700
www.adl.org

National Abortion and Repro-
    ductive Rights Action League
    (NARAL)
1156 15th Street, NW, Suite 700
Washington, DC 20005
202–973–3000
202–973–3096 fax
www.naral.org

Southern Poverty Law Center
PO Box 548
Montgomery, AL 36101
334–264–0286
334–264–0629 fax
www.splcenter.org
Keeps a close eye on hate groups
and militias with the Militia Task
Force and Klanwatch.

Refuse and Resist!
305 Madison Avenue,
    Suite 1166
New York, NY 10165
212–713–5657
www.walrus.com/~resist
A group of troublemakers that fight
it all—sexism, racism, homopho-
bia, censorship, and "compulsory
patriotism."

Senator Jesse Helms
U.S. Senate
Washington, DC 20510
www.senate.gov/~helms/
E-Mail: *helms@helms.senate.gov*

Jesse Helms a.k.a. Jersse Herlms
*www.BigBangCom.com/
    herlmspg.htm*
Anti-Jesse Website with download-
able audio clips of anti-Jesse radio
show.

Gay and Lesbian Alliance
    Against Defamation
    (GLAAD)
150 West 26th Street, Suite 503
New York, NY 10001
212–807–1700
212–807–1806 fax
www.glaad.org

Invading the Beach at Greenwich, Connecticut

Best Beaches in the USA
www.petrix.com/beaches/index.html

Town of Greenwich Depart-
    ment of Parks and Recreation
Edward Bilek, Jr., Director
PO Box 2540
Greenwich, CT 06836
203–622–7814
203–622–6494 fax

Greenwich Chamber of
   Commerce
21 West Putnam Avenue
Greenwich, CT 06830
203–869–3500
www.futuris.net/greenwich

Payback Time

Revenge Unlimited
www.revengeunlimited.com
"For all your getting even needs."
Offers ideas, chat rooms, tools,
fashion tips, and a library of
resources for paybacks.

Crackers, the Corporate Crime-Fighting Chicken

E-mail: *WingIt9@aol.com*
Send your crime tips to Crackers!
Although still in retirement, he
loves to get mail.

Corporate Crime Reporter
Russell Mokhiber, Editor
1209 National Press Building
Washington, DC 20045
202–737–1680

Public Citizen
1600 20th Street, NW
Washington, DC 20009
202–588–1000
www.citizen.org
The consumer's eyes and ears in
Washington. Founded by Ralph

Nader to fight for safer drugs and
medical devices, cleaner and safer
energy sources, a cleaner environment, fair trade, and a more open
and democratic government.

The CEO Challenge

Corporate Watch
www.corpwatch.org/home.html
Corporate Watch exposes corporate
greed by documenting social, political, economic, and environmental
impacts of transnational corporations and strives to build greater
democratic control over these companies.

Executive Paywatch
www.paywatch.org
A working families' guide to monitoring and curtailing the excessive
salaries, bonuses, and perks for
CEOs.

Ford Motor Company
313–322–3000
www.ford.com/us
Homepage of the company whose
CEO, Alex Trotman, accepted the
TV Nation CEO challenge and
changed the oil in a Ford Explorer.

Colgate-Palmolive
300 Park Avenue
New York, NY 10022
212–310–2000
www.colgate.com

Philip Morris
120 Park Avenue
New York, NY 10017
212–880–5000
www.philipmorris.com

Brian Anthony Harris Is Not Wanted

The Sentencing Project
www.sproject.com
Designed to provide resolution and information for those concerned with criminal justice and sentencing issues.

Federal Bureau of Investigation (FBI)
935 Pennsylvania Avenue
Washington, DC 20535–0001
202–324–3000
www.fbi.gov

Taxi

National Association for the Advancement of Colored People (NAACP), Washington Bureau
10025 Vermont Avenue, NW, Suite 1120
Washington, DC 20005
202–638–2269
410–521–4939
www.naacp.org

Slaves

The U.S. Constitution
www.house.gov/Constitution/ Constitution.html

Amendments to the Constitution
www.house.gov/Constitution/ Amend.html

The Emancipation Proclamation
www.nps.gov/ncro/anti/ emancipation.html

Museum of African Slavery
Pier M. Larson
Department of History
108 Weaver Building
The Pennsylvania State University
University Park, PA 16802–5500
814–863–8950
814–863–7840 fax
www3.la.psu.edu/~plarson/ smuseum
Discussion of slavery with links to other sites, information, and teaching resources.

The Underground Railroad
www.nps.gov/undergroundrr
National Park Service study on the Underground Railroad and research about how to commemorate the Railroad.

A Day with Dr. Death

Dr. Jack Kevorkian
4870 Lockhart
West Bloomfield, MI 48323

Oregon Death with Dignity Act Information
www.oregonrighttodie.org
Oregon is only state with legal assisted suicide.

Project on Death in America
Open Society Institute
400 West 59th Street
New York, NY 10019
212–548–0100
www.soros.org/death.html
Think tank/philanthropic group that studies death culture in America and works to improve the deaths of terminally ill patients.

Are You Prepared for Prison?

U.S. Bureau of Prisons
www.bop.gov

Abolish Capital Punishment Now
www.abolition-now.com
Contains information on wrongful executions, provides links to death penalty sites, hosts a death penalty forum, and explains what's wrong with the "eye for an eye" philosophy.

The Smoking Gun
www.thesmokinggun.com/
Another group of people that have been going to jail in larger numbers (though they may not be ready for it) are celebrities. This site features REAL celebrity legal documents.

I Want to Be an Argentinean

Falkland Islands Tourist Board
www.tourism.org.fk

Wales Tourist Board
www.tourism.wales.gov.uk

Consulate General of the Republic of Argentina in Chicago
205 North Michigan Avenue, Suite 4209
Chicago, IL 60601
312–819–2610
312–819–2612 fax
www.uic.edu/orgs/argentina/
E-mail: *argcchic@aol.com*

Argentine Embassy
1600 New Hampshire Avenue, NW
Washington, DC 20009
202–939–6400
www.mrecic.gov.ar/mrecic.htm

Tom Jones
www.catch.com/snack/tomjones
Fan site of singer Tom Jones that features a loop of the song "It's Not Unusual."

Junk Mail

U.S. Postal Service
www.usps.gov

Privacy Rights Clearinghouse
5384 Linda Vista Road, #306
San Diego, CA 92110
619–298–3398
619–298–5681 fax
www.privacyrights.org
E-mail: *prc@privacyrights.org*
Information on everything from
junk mail to caller ID to what to do
if your wallet is stolen.

Sabotage

The Steward
www.thesteward.hypenet.com
Online magazine for workers' and
human rights in Canada and the
U.S.

AFL-CIO (American Federation
    of Labor-Congress of Indus-
    trial Organizations)
815 16th Street, NW
Washington, DC 20006
202–637–5000
202–637–5058 fax
www.aflcio.org
Find out how to organize a union,
get a list of companies to boycott
and get union updates.

Dr. Katz, Professional Therapist
www.comedycentral.com/katz/
    index.html

Have an aggression therapy session
with Dr. Katz.

Yuri, Our *TV Nation* Spy

Russia Alive!
www.alincom.com/russ/index.htm
Provides information on all aspects
of Russian society, from art to business to politics to travel.

Virtual World of Spies and
    Intelligence
www.dreamscape.com/frankvad/
    covert.html
Will keep you informed of conspira-
cies, most wanted, intelligence
agencies, internet crime, law enforcement, military, terrorist activities, and
Area 51, among other secrets.

Paranoia.com
www.paranoia.com
Mainly concerned with First
Amendment issues but also deals
with conspiracy theories and other
various problems that come up in
an information society.

Mike's Missile

Russia Travel
www.russiatravel.com

The Kremlin
www.online.ru/sp/cominf/
    kremlin/kremlin.html
An online tour of the Kremlin.

American Civil Defense
Association
PO Box 1057
118 South Court Street
Starke, FL 32091
800–425–5397
904–964–5397
904–964–9641 fax
www.tacda.org
Even though the Cold War is over,
that doesn't mean there aren't dis-
asters to prepare for!

Haulin' Communism

The Communist Manifesto
downwithopp.com/lit/commie
Classic text written by Karl Marx
and Friedrich Engels about the
unfairness of capitalism and the
impending class war.

Truck Net
www.truck.net
Complete information source for
the trucking industry including
links, job listings, and a truck stop
directory.

The Johns of Justice

Occupational Safety and Health
Administration (OSHA)
U.S. Department of Labor
200 Constitution Avenue, NW
Washington, DC 20210
202–576–6339

202–576–7579 fax
www.osha.gov

Porta-John of America
50633 Ryan Road
Utica, MI 48317
888-PORTA-JOHN (767–8256)
www.toilets.com
E-mail: *pja@ic.net*
Supplier of portable toilets just in
case you want to have your own
Johns of Justice.

National Kidney Foundation
30 East 33rd Street, Suite 1100
New York, NY 10016
212–889–2210
212–779–0068 fax
www.kidney.org

With Neighbors Like These

Serial Killers
www.mayhem.net (then link to
serial killers page)
Webpage dedicated to serial killers
that ranks them by number of people they have killed.

Welcome Wagon
*www.cuc.com/ctg/cgi-bin/
WelcomeWagon/Home/*

Health Care Olympics

Ask Dr. Weil
cgi.pathfinder.com/drweil
Health guru Dr. Weil answers all

your health questions and does live Webcasts.

Helping People Survive Online
login.samart.co.th/~hps/tbhealth.htm
Ultimate Guide to alternative medicines.

Association for Responsible Medicine
PO Box 270986
Tampa, FL 33688
813–933–6236
www.a-r-m.org
E-mail: *armxd@sprynet.com*
Online magazine and group that helps protect patients from malpractice.

Doctors Without Borders USA
6 East Ninth Street, 8th Floor
New York, NY 10016
212–679–6800
212–679–7016 fax
www.dwb.org/
This organization has programs in Cuba to increase awareness of AIDS/HIV in young people aged 15 to 24 and to improve water sanitation.

Project InfoMed
United Services Agency, Inc.
PO Box 450
Santa Clara, CA 95052
www.igc.apc.org/cubasoli/

Provides medical information and informational tools, such as computers and modems, to health care providers in Cuba.

Destination Cuba
www.lonelyplanet.com/dest/car/cub.htm
Helpful Website that gives all the information one would need or want if traveling to Cuba.

Attractions Canada
attractions.infocan.gc.ca
Canada information page that includes news, general information, national forecasts, and links.

Cobb County
Common Cause
www.commoncause.org/

Official Friends of Newt
www.newt.org
Fan club of Newt Gingrich. Worth checking out to try to figure out what they are all about.

Newt's Page
www.house.gov/gingrich
Find out what Newt's up to on his official Congressional homepage.

Making Peace with Pizza
Amnesty International
322 Eighth Avenue
New York, NY 10001

1–800–AMNESTY (266–3789)
212–807–8400
212–627–1451 fax
www.amnesty.org
Amnesty is interested solely in protection of human rights, crossing
the boundaries of nations and
ideologies.

Human Rights Watch
350 Fifth Avenue, 34th Floor
New York, NY 10118
212–216–1200
212–736–1300 fax
www.hrw.org
Human Rights Watch aims to protect the human rights of people
around the world by working with
victims and activists to prevent discrimination, uphold political freedom, protect people from
inhumane conduct in wartime, and
to bring offenders to justice.

Pizza Hut
www.pizzahut.com

Bosnia 101
*www.taponline.com/tap/life/
newz/bosnia/index.html*
This site helps the layman understand what exactly is going on in
Bosnia.

State Department Information
*www.state.gov/www/regions/eur/
bosnia/index.html*

State Department page called
"Establishing a Durable Peace in
Bosnia and Herzegovina."

Yugo Next
*home.stlnet.com/~jimpotts/
yugonext.htm*
This site contains photographs of
artwork incorporating Yugo cars.

We Hire Our Own Lobbyist
National Lobbyist Directory
PO Box 18416
Capitol Hill Station
Denver, CO 80218–0416
www.lobbyistdirectory.com
Offers state-by-state directories of
lobbyists so you can understand
who gets the ear of your
representatives.

House of Representatives
www.house.gov

Senate
www.senate.gov

Congress phone:
202–225–3121

Congressional Record
*thomas.loc.gov/home/r105query.
html*

Whiny White Guys
Natural Resources Conservation
Service

14th and Independence
  Avenues, SW, Room 6218S
Washington, DC 20250
202–720–5626
www.nrcs.usda.gov

National Coalition of Free Men
PO Box 129
Manhasset, NY 11030
www.ncfm.org
This site has pro-male readings and information on the group's possible class action suit to be brought on behalf of divorced men.

National Organization for Men
11 Park Place, Suite 1116
New York, NY 10007
212–686–6253
www.tnom.com
"To protect men's rights and prevent the further erosion of men's status."

The Censored *TV* Nation

The Free Speech Policy Group
11 Peabody Terrace, Suite 2003
Cambridge, MA 02138
www.policygroup.com
E-mail:*Freespeech@policygroup.com*
Nonprofit think tank that advocates the protection of First Amendment rights by monitoring state and federal legislation as well as court decisions intended to restrict these rights.

Fairness and Accuracy in
  Reporting (FAIR)
130 West 25th Street
New York, NY 10001
212–633–6700
212–727–7668 fax
www.fair.org
Find out what the media isn't telling you by visiting this Website and their magazine, *Extra!*

The FCC's V-Chip Homepage
www.fcc.gov/vchip
E-mail: *Vchip@fcc.gov*
The Federal Communication Commission's page about the V-chip, the technology that will allow blocking certain programs from being received by one's TV. Also includes information on the TV rating system.

Miscellaneous

American Civil Liberties Union
  (ACLU)
125 Broad Street, 18th Floor
New York, NY 10004
212–549–2500
212–344–3318 fax
www.aclu.org
Protects everyone's First Amendment rights as well as rights to equal protection and due process.

Boycott Nike! Just Do It!
www.geocities.com/athens/
  acropolis/5232

Canada-based site that discusses in detail the progress of boycotts and actions against Nike's unfair labor practices. Includes a letter of protest to print and send to Nike's CEO, Phil Knight.

Bureau of Labor Statistics
Division of Information
    Services
2 Massachusetts Avenue, NE,
    Room 2860
Washington, DC 20212
202–606–5886
202–606–7890 fax
stats.bls.gov
Fact-finding agency for the federal government in the field of labor and economic statistics.

Campaign for Labor Rights
1247 E Street, SE
Washington, DC 20003
www.compugraph.com/clr
Mobilizes local support in the United States and Canada by building bridges between local activists and major organizations around the world.

Citizens for Corporate Accountability and Individual Rights
    (CCAIR)
1750 Ocean Park Boulevard
Santa Monica, CA 90405
310–392–0522
310–392–8874 fax

E-mail: *CCAIR@consumer-
    watchdog.com*
A national organization dedicated to raising public awareness about the dangers of tort reform, supporting efforts to stop and repeal tort reform laws, and instill in the public a new appreciation for the importance of this country's civil justice system.

Co-op America
1612 K Street, NW, Suite 600
Washington, DC 20006
800–58–GREEN
202–872–5307
202–331–8166 fax
www.coopamerica.org
Provides economic strategies, organizing power, and practical tools for businesses and individuals to address today's social and environmental problems and make significant improvements through the economic system.

Equal Employment Opportunity
    Commission (EEOC)
1801 L Street, NW
Washington, DC 20507
202–663–4900
202–663–4994 fax
www.eeoc.gov

Electronic Activist
www.berkshire.net/~ifas/activist

Provides e-mail address directory of Congresspeople, state governments, and media entities—information every online activist needs!

Global Exchange
2017 Mission Street, #303
San Francisco, CA 94110
415-255-7296
415-255-7498 fax
www.globalexchange.org
San Francisco-based nonprofit group that addresses human rights and economic justice issues.

Green Party
PO Box 100
Blodgett Mills, NY 13738
607-756-4211
www.greens.org/usa
Nader in 2000? Maybe. . . This Website helps you prepare by providing information on fielding ballot initiatives, organizing local Green groups and working on local environmental issues.

Institute for Global
   Communications
www.igc.org/igc
Created ten years ago to assist progressive movements by providing and developing computer networking and publishing tools. Links to a number of progressive groups through PeaceNet, EcoNet, Conflict-Net, LaborNet, and WomensNet.

International Brotherhood of
   Teamsters
25 Louisiana Avenue, NW
Washington, DC 20001
1-888-IBT-1111 (528-1111)
202-624-6832 fax
www.teamster.org
The Teamsters is the union everyone knows. They fight for better jobs and futures for all working people.

National Labor Relations Board
1099 14th Street, NW
Washington, DC 20570
202-273-3890
202-273-4266 fax
www.nlrb.gov
Federal agency that exists to administer the Labor Relations Act, the law governing relations between labor unions and the employers whose operations affect interstate commerce.

Project Vote Smart
129 NW 4th Street, Suite 204
Corvallis, OR 97330
541-754-2746
541-754-2747 fax
1-800-622-SMART
   (622-7627) (Voter's Research
   Hotline)
www.vote-smart.org
Tracks the performance of elected officials from the state to the fed-

eral level. Also includes helpful information on issues and free government publications and reports.

Sweatshop Watch
720 Market Street, 5th Floor
San Francisco, CA 94102
www.sweatshopwatch.org
This organization exists solely to educate consumers in a variety of ways about sweatshops in order to eliminate exploitation of garment workers.

UNITE!
1710 Broadway
New York, NY 10019
212–265–7000
www.uniteunion.org
Union that represents workers in Canada, the United States, and Puerto Rico and has taken a lead in organizing new workers and fighting against sweatshops and corporate greed.

United Auto Workers (UAW)
8000 East Jefferson
Detroit, MI 48214

1–800–2–GET–UAW
   (1–800–243–8829)
313–926–5000
1–800–387–0538 Canada
www.uaw.org
Union that includes people who make everything from planes to toy trains to cars, as well as state, county, and local government workers and hospital and university workers.

The White House
1600 Pennsylvania Avenue
Washington, DC 20500
202–456–1414
www.whitehouse.gov

To reach Michael Moore and Kathleen Glynn, contact:

Dog Eat Dog Films
PO Box 831
Radio City Station
New York, NY 10101
www.dogeatdogfilms.com
E-mail: *Dogfilms@aol.com*

Acknowledgments

This book, like the show, would not have been possible without the hard work of many individuals.

Our deepest gratitude goes to Michelle Johnston for her ability to create order out of chaos. Although Michelle was never on staff at *TV Nation*, she has an encyclopedic memory of every episode and, while we found that to be really scary, it sure came in handy.

Melanie Neilson was an associate producer and segment producer on *TV Nation*. She enthusiastically came back and helped us organize the existing material and research into a comprehensive library of *TV Nation* information.

To jump start our memory, Joanne Doroshow, the coordinating producer from the show, interviewed a number of the staff and recorded their war stories about the segments we shot for *TV Nation*.

Our staff at Dog Eat Dog Films led by Barbara Moss contributed fact-checking, Internet searching, copying, running, and endless other activities in the making of this book.

Thanks to our agent, Mort Janklow, and everyone in his office. Our gratitude goes to Fiona Hallowell, our editor at HarperCollins, for her calm exterior (we're sure she has been screaming inside), and to our advocate and number one fan, Susan Weinberg, who runs HarperPerennial.

As far as the show itself goes, we were very lucky to have worked with so many great people, including Jerry Kupfer, supervising producer extraordinaire, and the writers: Ann Cohen, John Derevlany, Francis Gasparini, Jay Martel, Steve Sherrill, and Eric Zicklin. Much of what you've read in this book is the result of their work. They cannot be thanked enough for their brilliant ideas. You should keep an eye out for their names in the future as we're sure this will not be the last time you see the fruits of their talent. Thanks also to Randy Cohen, Chris Kelly, and Jeff Stilson who showed us that, indeed, tragedy plus time equals comedy.

The army of producing talent that carried out these ideas includes: Andy Aaron, Frances Alswang, Kent Alterman, Jim Czarnecki, Patrick Farrelly, Paco de Onís, Immy Humes, Natalie Jason, Kate O'Callaghan, Geoff O'Connor, David Van Taylor, Pam Yates, David Wald, Subrata De, Helen Demeranville, Gideon Evans, Holley Knaus, Tia Lessin, Pearl Lieberman, Peri Muldofsky, Brooke Runnette, Haydeé Sabogal, Adrienne Salisbury, Robert Wilhelm, and Roger Williams. Their incredible work, always behind the camera, made every one of these stories priceless.

TV Nation, like most non-fiction, is finally created in the editing room. Thanks to all of our crack editors: Pamela Scott Arnold, Paula Heredia, Kristen Huntley, Jay Keuper, Peter Kinoy, Tim Squyres, Wendey Stanzler, Daisy Wright, David Zieff, and others.

Brian Danitz and Francisco Latorre were our regular camera and sound team, but there were many others across the country that shot footage and recorded sound for us on a day's notice— sometimes on an hour's notice. Veronica Moore responded to our fan mail—both regular mail and E-mail—and continues to do so at *TVNatFans@aol.com*. Kathleen Egan, Wendy Rowland, Susan Shorey, and Gretchen Schwarz provided personal assistance and organization to the producers, and consistently kept the network junior executives away from us.

Thanks to "the suits" who made *TV Nation* a reality: Jon Feltheimer, Eric Tannenbaum, Jocelyn Freid, and Steve Tann at Columbia TriStar Television; Michael Jackson (now head of Channel Four Television in the U.K.); Warren Littlefield, Kevin Reilly, and David Nevins at NBC; and John Matoian at Fox (now head of HBO Films).

Finally, we must recognize and thank the *TV Nation* correspondents:

Rusty Cundieff, for taking his slaves line-dancing; Janeane Garofalo, for jumping in the ocean and for confessing her sins; Karen Duffy, our good luck charm and a force the likes of which we've never seen; Ben Hamper, for his "smallness"; Merrill Markoe, for her incredible wit; Louis Theroux, for his willingness to go in front of the camera; Steven Wright, for keeping us laughing; Jonathan Katz, for listening; Roy Sekoff, for riding that sludge train; and, of course, for sheer comic inspiration (without even trying), Louis Bruno and Luciano Dellacaprini of the Bronx.

To all of these individuals and the three hundred others that worked on the show, we express our respect and gratitude for their help in making a program that broke a lot of new ground.

Finally, to our daughter, Natalie, we owe special thanks. She waited for dinner, endured endless discussion about the show, the studio, and the staff, and stayed up late keeping her mom company in the final days of the book.

Michael Moore & Kathleen Glynn

July 1998

MICHAEL MOORE

Downsize This!

Random Threats from an Unarmed American

PAN BOOKS £7.99

From the best-selling author of *Stupid White Men*, the creator of *TV Nation* and the award-winning most popular documentary of all time *Roger and Me*, comes a classic title by Michael Moore for all you disillusioned, political abstainees who are working longer hours for less pay and have *had enough*.

Michael Moore has established himself as an internationally renowned social and political commentator; as someone who just won't shut up, go away, or otherwise do what political and corporate fat cats would like him to do.

Nothing but the truth is sacred in this hilarious screed on the state of the USA. With chapter headings such as 'Why Doesn't General Motors Sell Crack?' setting the tone for a biting indictment of American corporate politics, Moore's take-no-prisoners attitude is brutally funny, insightful and irrepressible. Michael Moore lifts the veil on the people who set themselves up as our role models and hysterically exposes their vulnerable underbellies.

'America has an irrepressible new humorist in the tradition of Mark Twain . . . he is Michael Moore'
New York Times

'Michael Moore deserves one of those Genius grants so he can take on any subject of his choosing'
New York Post

OTHER BOOKS

AVAILABLE FROM PAN MACMILLAN
